Scorpio

OCTOBER 23–NOVEMBER 22

2007

JOVE BOOKS, NEW YORK

THE BERKLEY PUBLISHING GROUP
Published by the Penguin Group
Penguin Group (USA) Inc.
375 Hudson Street, New York, New York 10014, USA
Penguin Group (Canada), 90 Eglinton Avenue East, Suite 700, Toronto, Ontario M4P 2Y3, Canada
(a division of Pearson Penguin Canada Inc.)
Penguin Books Ltd., 80 Strand, London WC2R 0RL, England
Penguin Group Ireland, 25 St. Stephen's Green, Dublin 2, Ireland (a division of Penguin Books Ltd.)
Penguin Group (Australia), 250 Camberwell Road, Camberwell, Victoria 3124, Australia
(a division of Pearson Australia Group Pty. Ltd.)
Penguin Books India Pvt. Ltd., 11 Community Centre, Panchsheel Park, New Delhi—110 017, India
Penguin Group (NZ), Cnr. Airborne and Rosedale Roads, Albany, Auckland 1310, New Zealand
(a division of Pearson New Zealand Ltd.)
Penguin Books (South Africa) (Pty.) Ltd., 24 Sturdee Avenue, Rosebank, Johannesburg 2196,
South Africa

Penguin Books Ltd., Registered Offices: 80 Strand, London WC2R 0RL, England

The publishers regret that they cannot answer individual letters
requesting personal horoscope information.

2007 TOTAL HOROSCOPE: SCORPIO

PRINTING HISTORY
Jove edition / June 2006

Copyright © 1977, 1978, 1979, 1980, 1981, 1982 by Grosset & Dunlap, Inc.
Copyright © 1983, 1984 by Charter Communications, Inc.
Copyright © 1985, 1986 by The Berkley Publishing Group.
Copyright © 1987, 1988, 1989, 1990, 1991, 1992, 1993, 1994, 1995, 1996,
1997, 1998, 1999, 2000, 2001, 2002, 2003, 2004, 2005, 2006 by Penguin Group (USA) Inc.
Cover art by Christian Dente.
Cover design by Erika Fusari.
Astrological perspectives by Michael Lutin.

ISBN: 0-515-14110-0

JOVE®
Jove Books are published by The Berkley Publishing Group,
a division of Penguin Group (USA) Inc.
375 Hudson Street, New York, New York 10014.
Jove and the "J" design are registered trademarks of Penguin Group (USA) Inc.

PRINTED IN THE UNITED STATES OF AMERICA

10   9   8   7   6   5   4   3   2   1

CONTENTS

♏

MESSAGE TO SCORPIO

Dear Scorpio,

Yours is a nature of dark intensity and swirling passions. Sexual magnetism pervades your whole being and you have a serious interest in your sex life. The rumors and myths have it that Scorpio has the best love life of all the signs, but it's not always true. Scorpios develop early and experiment in many ways emotionally when they are very young. They often have many sexual experiences in their search for an ideal mate, one who can satisfy their intense needs. When they find one, they are faithful, honorable, and usually monogamous. However, love life can be a problem. Scorpios may have to rechannel their drives and fit them into realistic life patterns, effecting a total change.

But the passion for life never dies. No matter what your private life is like, you have a thirst for love and a desire for survival that makes you irresistible. Sometimes, when people hear you're Scorpio, they act a little afraid. It's usually a ruse to cover up their titillation and excitement and secret hope that you'll seduce them. You are stirred by primitive passions that are the basis for your sexual orientation, creative drives, and need for self-expression. No other sign has such a profound instinct for survival and reproduction. Out of the abyss of your emotions come a thousand creations, each one with a life of its own, each one like an incomprehensible abstract painting.

So you are a passionate lover and a prolific artist. Often your eyes snap and crackle with the dark energy of your whole being. When you fix your interest on someone or something, you become obsessed.

Nothing, but nothing, can stop you from winning your lover or achieving your goal. You are competitive and determined, fortified with enough endurance and stamina to outlive any enemy, physical or psychological. When challenged you can spit in the eye of death and pursue your ambitions despite every threat, warning, or obstacle in your path. You simply cannot be deterred. You know when to wait. When you smell danger, you retreat into a cave. Your eyes peer out of the darkness. You count your losses and recoup your strength. When the moment is right you reemerge, stronger than ever, healed and invincible.

You are friendly, considerate, and generous. Your strength and courage are inspiring qualities that people around you admire and call upon when they are in trouble. You are fiercely loyal and don't like anyone to fool around with your mate. You're jealous, possessive, and dangerously aroused if you think people are taking advantage of you. You prefer not to fight openly because you know how bloody the battle can get. You are not afraid to fight, however, and your life is often intensely gripped in life-and-death situations. You remain in a constant state of readiness and awareness, like an animal that sleeps with one eye open.

When the fight is actually on, you'll do what is necessary to win. You'll be devious, ruthless, and cruel. You'll save a bitter, sarcastic remark for the right moment, then hit your opponent with a barb that pierces deep and strikes its deathly blow. In this sense you have a cold streak. You keep your emotions under control, then act quickly and decisively in any situation that calls for striking while the iron is hot.

Sometimes you smell danger when it isn't there, which causes trouble in many of your relationships. You are cautious, suspicious, and deeply aware of your position with respect to other people. When you think there's a threat, you can become vindictive, treacherous, and filled with venom.

But isn't all this a little dramatic? Frankly, yes. Scorpios' actual lives are not smoldering and steeping like volcanoes and jungles. Most of the time you lead simple, normal lives. You work, raise families, have relationships, keep house. But Scorpio's dramatic intensity is there nonetheless. Creative self-expression is a must. Without it, you will create intrigues and complexities or work all that energy back in on yourself as illness or disease.

You are an ardent and faithful lover—there is no doubt about that. When you are truly in love you can be tender, compassionate, forgiving. Otherwise, sex can be a selfish and shallow affair. In some areas of your life, you cut people out without a thought and never forget wrongs that are done to you. But on the whole, you don't like to lose touch or control of those you love. People can be just as shocked by your greed as they are excited by it. You have to develop a spiritual side if you are not to get lost in self-indulgence and materialistic pursuits.

You are a hardheaded realist. You are generous with your belongings provided there's enough for you. For those you love you are a divine provider. Anything they want, you are prepared to offer. You delight in satisfying their desires. When it comes to money, you are generally lucky. You believe in luck and because you do, it happens to you. You are certainly not an idler who sits around hoping for the best. When you want something, you are ambitious, persistent, thorough, efficient, and hardworking. But you believe in an overall luck in finances, and as a result you rarely go without. You often rise to great heights, financially or otherwise, because you unite drive and magnetism. It's hard for people to resist or refuse you.

You are often suspicious of those around you. Either your siblings posed some limitation on you which you had to conquer, or some adolescent problem made you grow up and look at the world through the eyes of a determined realist. Whatever the original cause, the result is your amazing power to perceive people for what they are. Your capacity for penetrating analysis is unsurpassable. It will be of help to you in any creative career field.

You generally don't want to be tied down to home and family, although your primitive territorial instincts often drive you toward claiming a partner and mating. You don't want your domestic scene to be a humdrum, run-of-the-mill one, and often you set a scandalous example for your neighbors to follow.

You're a strict parent who is often undone by your kids. It's hard for children to understand your single-minded, often rough demeanor. You are sometimes caught between your need to satisfy the desires of your ego and your responsibilities to the youngsters. This can lead to guilt, deception, and disillusion which can only be resolved by time and maturity.

No matter what you're involved in, you can be a ferocious fanatic. You can work like a fiend, especially on projects that are new and exciting and that tap your creativity, originality, and inventiveness. You're naturally sound of body and of a strong, healthy constitution. You can imagine the worst, because you're a person of extremes—extreme highs and lows, extreme obsessions, extreme fantasies. Although you possess remarkable physical endurance and resilience, you tend to magnify your ills and, through worry, aggravate them. Your sex organs, intestines, and organs of elimination are vitally connected with all your other glands and your body in general. By reflex you are physically joined to the throat, spine, heart, and circulatory system. Physical and psychic functions are united through your glands. Acceptance of your sexual identity is one key to health and success.

You can draw the best and richest resources out of people. In your relationships you can be parasitic or inspiring; you can take life or give it. You tend to marry for money or to enrich your life somehow. Your best partners are conservative, gentle, faithful, honorable, firm—lovers who will support you on any level. You need someone who loves pleasure and can see you through brooding and bad moods. You can provide a strong sense of renewal and transformation for your partner. Your arrival may mark a permanent revision in your mate's life, the closing of some doors forever and the opening of new ones.

Your sexual experimentalism is a usual part of your development. Your ethical standards are traditional. But your baser interest in superficial, even tawdry sex, contradicts your need for stable, monogamous relationships and high moral codes. The religious principles of your ancestors often play a role in your life. So you must come to terms with the philosophical teachings of your childhood while striking out on your own to find yourself.

You are a proud, noble creature whose aim is to shine and be great at whatever you do. You need the spotlight. Show business and sports attract you. You look up to people who sparkle and express their creative selves with flair and style. Style is something you've got plenty of yourself. You like to look good, and you project yourself with flair and drama. You're a great host and entertainer. But you are a creature of the night with a great need for intimacy, secrecy, and intrigue. You are often outgoing, helpful, and friendly, a humble and earnest servant to your friends. You strive for honor above all things. Yet it is often said—and rightly so—that a Scorpio never tells everything. There are things about you no one will ever know. They may be simple, unimportant, silly things, but they're all yours.

You may look to someone around you for direction, money, focus, or criticism, but basically you are a self-directed creature with a will of steel. Relationships, both personal and professional, often haunt you, because you chase and run away from them at the same time. You need another human being desperately. You long to lock horns on the battlefield of love and sex, and your desire and passion for the touch of a loving hand are hungers you cannot escape. You have a burning desire to create life, to deliver yourself into another human being's love. But it's hard for you to surrender your identity to another, so you collide and flee, only to be drawn again into contact. This obsessiveness forces you to re-examine yourself and your desire for an intimate relationship.

You are a dominant figure who makes an excellent partner. You will is strong and your demands are great. You like to rule, loathe criticism, and seek always to be the master of the situation. Although you manipulate and control, and operate on all levels at once—conscious and unconscious—you are a dauntless hero with a magician's touch for turning away evil.

You are attracted to mystery with a bloodhound's nose for solving it. No clues escape your scrutiny. No suspects elude your penetrating gaze and analytical mind. You are a fearsome adversary, an eloquent cross-examiner. When you sniff out a lead, you're on the track and never rest till the case is solved.

Your problems are always solved with one pure quality: strength of purpose. You can blind your eyes to facts and latch on to fantastic obsessions, unrealistic schemes, and impossible desires. Your rigid stamina and unshakable faith often lead you to victory anyway. But there are moments when you're down and nobody can pull you out of the mud of your own depressions. Loving partners may try, but you may strike out at them and send them away. Nobody can save you from yourself at these times, except you. When you come to the conclusion that something is bad for you, you can eradicate it swiftly from your life, painlessly and forever, without blinking twice. But it takes you a while to get to that point, because you like to pass endurance tests.

Of all the Scorpio traits, there is one that is most inspiring. It is the quality of personality that sets you apart and makes you the extraordinary creature you are. It makes you the bravest of all your astrological cousins and puts you in a category with mystics and magicians of all ages. This is the Scorpio capacity for total transformation—what is termed metamorphosis.

You may have read somewhere that there are two types of Scorpio—the scorpion and the eagle.

The scorpion is capable of biting itself and dying from its own venom. So watch out for your baser instincts of revenge and bitterness. But there is honor and nobility in the scorpion's nature. If you try to escape from your animal self and pretend it isn't there, it's possible that you will poison your whole system. The animal drives get the credit for that remarkable instinct you have for survival—the driving, unintelligent, uncommunicating, unthinking reaction to danger that makes you win in battle. The thirst for power is the danger here. Nobody is more capable of being carried away with power than Scorpio. Your instinct for survival could be magnified into a power hunger that would never stop, and you could go on drawing life from all who came near. Eventually you could engulf yourself in greed, desire, and lust, and even draw life from yourself.

The eagle is reputed to be the symbol of nobility. The bird flies over all, a transformed being representative of the higher side of Scorpio, the healer and magician. Scorpio has battled the forces of darkness and death, and won. He has confronted the illusions of danger and self-annihilation, and emerged supreme. Nothing frightens him because he has pierced his own fears and fantasies. He has faced himself and passed the ultimate test. He is the embodiment of truth and lives to heal the wounds of his fellow man. Fear and disease flee from him, for he has proved himself against visions and manifestations of evil. He has successfully and consciously survived personal crisis. Now he has wings on high in joyous celebration of victory.

But again, all this sounds a bit heavy and dramatic.

You don't really live in such tempestuous, mysterious existences, do you? Or do you? Scorpio wrestles with forces beyond the visible world, parts of the consciousness that are the outposts of the mind. Even if such battles are going on, how do you change from one kind of Scorpio to another? Is that kind of total change possible for anybody?

Yes. You are the one who can make the change more than anyone else. Scorpio has the capacity of the caterpillar to spin its own cocoon. You just spin and spin without knowing what will happen, if anything. You enter the cocoon consciously, willingly, facing the end of one existence without knowing anything about what lies ahead. All you have is the fact that you are alive and conscious and gifted with some brilliant something we will call intelligence. You have to have the courage to say good-bye to your old way of life, safe and sure and happy though it was, and step into that cocoon, and spin it shut right to the top. At that point nothing comes in. Nothing goes out. The past is over. For all intents and purposes everything seems dead.

Then amid the vacuum of uncertainty, from the darkness of doubt and dread, the cocoon is broken. Something has occurred. Can we call it miraculous? This is the meaning of Scorpio. From the hopelessness of despair and the inevitability of personal crisis, transformation can be achieved.

Michael Lutin

SCORPIO PREVIEW
OF THE 21st CENTURY

As the decade opens on a new century, indeed on a new millennium, the planets set the stage for change and challenge. Themes connecting present and future are in play. Already, planetary influences that emerged from the century just past are showing the drama unfolding in the twenty-first century. These influences reveal hidden paths and personal hints for achieving your potential—your message from the planets.

Scorpio individuals, ruled by the planets Pluto and Mars, are fired with purpose and enthusiasm as new cycles extend and expand your capacity for emotional, sexual, and spiritual rejuvenation. Your ruler Pluto, planet of transformation and growth, of sudden endings and beginnings, is in the idealistic sign of Sagittarius whose ruler Jupiter confers good luck and good fortune.

Pluto in Sagittarius to the year 2008 takes you on a significant journey of exploration and learning. Optimistic Sagittarius and enduring Scorpio combine to produce a vibrant life force. While Sagittarius exuberantly encourages taking chances, Scorpio shrewdly calculates the odds and plots strategy. When Sagittarius broadens the horizon, Scorpio imbues fresh experience with deep meaning.

The transit of Pluto in Sagittarius is especially important for Scorpio finances, as it activates and develops the section of your horoscope that has to do with money and material resources. This section is your second house, the house of finances. And the transits of benevolent planet Jupiter and taskmaster planet Saturn interact to affect your finances.

With Jupiter in Cancer, a water sign like yours, your ambition is strong, bolstered by the mental toughness of Saturn in Gemini into June 2003. Jupiter in Leo is a dramatic period with potential risks because of the stubborn yet explosive nature of both Leo and Scorpio.

When Jupiter transits Virgo until early autumn 2004, humanitarian aims prevail, leading to important intellectual output and worthy social service. And Saturn in Cancer June 2003 to July 2005 highlights career opportunity, achievement, and prestige.

Jupiter visits Libra, your twelfth house of secret wisdom and knowledge, from early autumn of 2004 to late October of 2005. With Jupiter in Libra comes deep self-exploration and a newfound sense of who you are and what you want.

Jupiter is in your sign of Scorpio, your first house, from October 26 of 2005 to November 23 of 2006. With Jupiter in your sign, you present a new persona, a new you, to the world. But with Saturn in Leo from July 2005 into September 2007, there can be a tug-of-war between personal ambition and public spiritedness.

Jupiter in Sagittarius late November 2006 to late December 2007 can bring prosperity to the astute Scorpio. And with Saturn in Virgo from September 2007 into 2010, your luck is improved if you know how to ride the wave of your own good fortune.

Uranus, planet of innovation, is in the inspirational sign of Pisces from late 2003 into year 2010. Pisces, another water sign like yours, brings a spiritual theme to forceful Scorpio emotions and ideas. A flowering of creativity bursts forth. And your Scorpio powers of healing change are brought to the fore.

Neptune, planet of imagination and vision, is in Aquarius throughout the first decade of the twenty-first century and beyond into year 2012. Neptune's long cycle inspires the Scorpio love of investigation, turning you on to the mysteries of life.

THE CUSP-BORN SCORPIO

Are you *really* a Scorpio? If your birthday falls during the third to fourth week of October, at the beginning of Scorpio, will you still retain the traits of Libra, the sign of the Zodiac before Scorpio? What if you were born late in November—are you more Sagittarius than Scorpio? Many people born at the edge, or cusp, of a sign have difficulty determining exactly what sign they are. If you are one of these people, here's how you can figure it out, once and for all.

Consult the table on page 17. Find the year you were born, and then note the day. The table will tell you the precise days on which the Sun entered and left your sign for the year of your birth. If you were born at the beginning or end of Scorpio, yours is a lifetime reflecting a process of subtle transformation. Your life on Earth will symbolize a significant change in consciousness, for you are either about to enter a whole new way of living or you are leaving one behind.

If you were born at the beginning of Scorpio, you may want to read the horoscope book for Libra as well as Scorpio, for Libra holds the keys to much of the complexity of your spirit and reflects many of your hidden weaknesses, secret sides, and unspoken wishes.

You have a keen way of making someone feel needed and desired, whether you care deeply or not. Sex is a strong directive in your life. You might turn your charm and seductiveness toward gaining a merely superficial relationship. You could use your sexual magnetism and love magic to win people over for the sheer purpose of being seen as partnered in a respectable couple.

You can love with an almost fatal obsession, a bigger-than-both-of-you type thing. You may blind your eyes to basic incompatibilities just to keep the peace in a relationship—then suddenly declare war.

No one in the whole Zodiac is as turned on to the passions of life as you are. You can survive any crisis, for deep in your spirit lie the seeds of immortality and you know it. Above all you are the symbol that life goes on—the personification of awakening passion.

If you were born at the end of Scorpio, you may want to read the horoscope book for Sagittarius as well as Scorpio. You are the symbol of the human mind awakening to its higher capabilities. What you are leaving behind is greed, blind desire, and shallow lust, as you awaken to your own ability to learn, to create, and to understand.

You want to travel, see new places, see how people live, figure yourself out, acquire knowledge—yet you are often not quite ready to take the plunge. When you shift your behavior patterns significantly and permanently, new worlds open up and you turn on to immortality and the infinite possibilities of your own mind.

THE CUSPS OF SCORPIO

DATES SUN ENTERS SCORPIO
(LEAVES LIBRA)

October 23 every year from 1900 to 2010,
except for the following:

October 22	October 24			
1992	1902	1911	1923	1943
1996	03	14	27	47
2000	06	15	31	51
2004	07	18	35	55
2008	10	19	39	59

DATES SUN LEAVES SCORPIO
(ENTERS SAGITTARIUS)

November 22 every year from 1900 to 2010,
except for the following:

November 21		November 23		
1976	1993	1902	1915	1931
80	1996	03	19	35
84	2000	07	23	39
88	2004	10	27	43
92	2008	11		

SCORPIO RISING:
YOUR ASCENDANT

Could you be a "double" Scorpio? That is, could you have Scorpio as your Rising sign as well as your Sun sign? The tables on pages 20–21 will tell you Scorpios what your Rising sign happens to be. Just find the hour of your birth, then find the day of your birth, and you will see which sign of the Zodiac is your Ascendant, as the Rising sign is called.

Your Ascendant, or Rising sign, modifies your basic Sun sign personality, and it affects the way you act out the daily predictions for your Sun sign. If your Rising sign is indeed Scorpio, what follows is a description of its effects on your horoscope. If your Rising sign is some other sign of the Zodiac, you may wish to read the horoscope book for that sign as well.

With Scorpio Rising, look to planets Mars and Pluto, the rulers of Scorpio. You have the tremendous energy of Mars and the implacable avenging power of Pluto, which together make you a tower of forcefulness. Mars accentuates action, Pluto signifies spiritual development. You can be a bold crusader for truth, a relentless foe of injustice. Or you can be bitter, sarcastic, vengeful, and capable of harboring destructive impulses toward the self as well as toward society.

There may be dramatic extremes in the conduct of your life. You will obsessively pursue a goal, be consumed by it, seemingly drop it, then move on to a new sphere of endeavor and influence. Pluto, the planet of transformation, emphasizes beginnings and endings in a continuum of development. The marked variations in your lifestyle may be an expression of that cycle of change. Your capacity to learn from experience is immense, and this ability enables you to rise to great positions during a lifetime.

Control is a byword for Scorpio Rising. Whether it is control over self, control over others, or control through others, you are a great strategist. In your arsenal are such contradictory traits as subtlety, intensity, selfishness, self-sacrifice, ruthlessness, possessiveness, aloofness, impulsiveness, determination. Linked to your need for control is your love of power. You have enough passion and endurance to attain power, and then to use it to change your environment.

As much as you like to dominate, you hate being dominated. You will go to great lengths to escape being trapped in a chafing relationship or situation. People may see you as perverse and self-seeking, ready for flight or fight. You hate to lose, whether the conquest is an argument, or a cause, or a lover. Your anger and jealousy are renowned. You get deeply involved, though your manner can be impersonal. You have a penchant for solitude and secrecy, so people often think you are introverted and shy—until they get to know you intimately.

Your potential for inner growth and external change is almost unlimited. A constantly developing spiritual component puts you in touch with the mysterious forces of the universe. Your energy and drive are rooted in the psychosexual nature of humankind, which is indeed a basic organizer of all human effort and thought. On an operational level, your initiative and inventiveness give you a practical side that often obscures the depths of your being.

Stamina and transformation are key words for Scorpio Rising. You can change situations for good or bad, for selfless service or self-promotion. You can lead the struggle for survival and creativity.

RISING SIGNS FOR SCORPIO

Hour of Birth*	Day of Birth		
	October 23–27	October 26–31	November 1–5
Midnight	Leo	Leo	Leo
1 AM	Leo	Leo; Virgo 10/30	Virgo
2 AM	Virgo	Virgo	Virgo
3 AM	Virgo	Virgo	Virgo; Libra 11/5
4 AM	Libra	Libra	Libra
5 AM	Libra	Libra	Libra
6 AM	Libra	Libra; Scorpio 10/30	Scorpio
7 AM	Scorpio	Scorpio	Scorpio
8 AM	Scorpio	Scorpio	Scorpio
9 AM	Sagittarius	Sagittarius	Sagittarius
10 AM	Sagittarius	Sagittarius	Sagittarius
11 AM	Sagittarius	Capricorn	Capricorn
Noon	Capricorn	Carpricorn	Capricorn
1 PM	Capricorn; Aquarius 10/26	Aquarius	Aquarius
2 PM	Aquarius	Aquarius	Pisces
3 PM	Pisces	Pisces	Pisces; Aries 11/5
4 PM	Aries	Aries	Aries
5 PM	Aries; Taurus 10/26	Aquarius	Aquarius
6 PM	Taurus	Taurus	Gemini
7 PM	Gemini	Gemini	Gemini
8 PM	Gemini	Gemini;	Cancer
9 PM	Cancer	Cancer	Cancer
10 PM	Cancer	Cancer	Cancer
11 PM	Leo	Leo	Leo

*Hour of birth given here is for Standard Time in any time zone. If your hour of birth was recorded in Daylight Saving Time, subtract one hour from it and consult that hour in the table above. For example, if you were born at 7 AM D.S.T., see 6 AM above.

Hour of Birth*	Day of Birth		
	November 6–11	November 12–16	November 17–23
Midnight	Leo	Leo; Virgo 11/15	Virgo
1 AM	Virgo	Virgo	Virgo
2 AM	Virgo	Virgo	Virgo; Libra 11/21
3 AM	Libra	Libra	Libra
4 AM	Libra	Libra	Libra
5 AM	Libra	Libra; Scorpio 11/14	Scorpio
6 AM	Scorpio	Scorpio	Scorpio
7 AM	Scorpio	Scorpio	Scorpio; Sagittarius 11/21
8 AM	Sagittarius	Sagittarius	Sagittarius
9 AM	Sagittarius	Sagittarius	Sagittarius
10 AM	Sagittarius	Capricorn	Capricorn
11 AM	Capricorn	Capricorn	Capricorn
Noon	Capricorn; Aquarius 11/10	Aquarius	Aquarius
1 PM	Aquarius	Aquarius	Pisces
2 PM	Pisces	Pisces	Pisces; Aries 11/21
3 PM	Aries	Aries	Aries
4 PM	Aries	Taurus	Taurus
5 PM	Taurus	Taurus	Gemini
6 PM	Gemini	Gemini	Gemini
7 PM	Gemini	Gemini; Cancer 11/16	Cancer
8 PM	Cancer	Cancer	Cancer
9 PM	Cancer	Cancer	Cancer; Leo 11/22
10 PM	Leo	Leo	Leo
11 PM	Leo	Leo	Leo

*See note on facing page.

LOVE AND RELATIONSHIPS

No matter who you are, what you do in life, or where your planets are positioned, you still need to be loved, and to feel love for other human beings. Human relationships are founded on many things: infatuation, passion, sex, guilt, friendship, and a variety of other complex motivations, frequently called love.

Relationships often start out full of hope and joy, the participants sure of themselves and sure of each other's love, and then end up more like a pair of gladiators than lovers. When we are disillusioned, bitter, and wounded, we tend to blame the other person for difficulties that were actually present long before we ever met. Without seeing clearly into our own natures we will be quite likely to repeat our mistakes the next time love comes our way.

Enter Astrology.

It is not always easy to accept, but knowledge of ourselves can improve our chances for personal happiness. It is not just by predicting when some loving person will walk into our lives, but by helping us come to grips with our failures and reinforce our successes.

Astrology won't solve all our problems. The escapist will ultimately have to come to terms with the real world around him. The hard-bitten materialist will eventually acknowledge the eternal rhythms of the infinite beyond which he can see or hear. Astrology does not merely explain away emotion. It helps us unify the head with the heart so that we can become whole individuals. It helps us define what it is we are searching for, so we can recognize it when we find it.

Major planetary cycles have been changing people's ideas about love and commitment, marriage, partnerships, and relationships. These cycles have affected virtually everyone in areas of personal involvement. Planetary forces point out upheavals and transformations occurring in all of society. The concept of marriage is being totally reexamined. Exactly what the changes will ultimately bring no one can tell. It is usually difficult to determine which direction society will take. One thing is certain: no man is an island. If the rituals and pomp of wedding ceremonies must be revised, then it will happen.

Social rules are being revised. Old outworn institutions are indeed crumbling. But relationships will not die. People are putting less stress on permanence and false feelings of security. The emphasis now shifts toward the union of two loving souls. Honesty, equality, and mutual cooperation are the goals in modern marriage. When these begin to break down, the marriage is in jeopardy. Surely there must be a balance between selfish separatism and prematurely giving up.

There is no doubt that astrology can establish the degree of compatibility between two human beings. Two people can share a common horizon in life but have quite different habits or basic interests. Two others might have many basic characteristics in common while needing to approach their goals from vastly dissimilar points of view. Astrology describes compatibility based on these assumptions.

It compares and contrasts through the fundamental characteristics that draw two people together. Although they could be at odds on many basic levels, two people could find themselves drawn together again and again. Sometimes it seems that we keep being attracted to the same type of individuals. We might ask ourselves if we have learned anything from our past mistakes. The answer is that there are qualities in people that we require and thus seek out time and time again. To solve that mystery in ourselves is to solve much of the dilemma of love, and so to help ourselves determine if we are approaching a wholesome situation or a potentially destructive one.

We are living in a very curious age with respect to marriage and relationships. We can easily observe the shifting social attitudes concerning the whole institution of marriage. People are seeking everywhere for answers to their own inner needs. In truth, all astrological combinations can achieve compatibility. But many relationships seem doomed before they get off the ground. Astrologically there can be too great a difference between the goals, aspirations, and personal outlook of the people involved. Analysis of both horoscopes must and will indicate enough major planetary factors to keep the two individuals together. Call it what you will: determination, patience, understanding, love—whatever it may be, two people have the capacity to achieve a state of fulfillment together. We all have different needs and desires. When it comes to choosing a mate, you really have to know yourself. If you know the truth about what you are really looking for, it will make it easier to find. Astrology is a useful, almost essential, tool to that end.

In the next chapter your basic compatibility with each of the twelve signs of the Zodiac is generalized. The planetary vibrations between you and an individual born under any given zodiacal sign suggest much about how you will relate to each other. Hints are provided about love and romance, sex and marriage so that you and your mate can get the most out of the relationship that occupies so important a role in your life.

SCORPIO:
YOU AND YOUR MATE

SCORPIO—ARIES

This is an exciting and dangerous combination. Aries makes you work, and you turn your Aries on, deep down at the most primitive levels of being. Instead of turning these interactions against yourselves and developing a diabolical and constantly escalating war, you can work them into a source of inspiration on fundamental sexual, emotional, creative, and practical levels.

You share the primary instincts for being: survival, life, death. When it comes to ambition, energy, and stamina, you are both unbeatable. You are both stubborn and strong-willed. You conflict in your views of openness and secrecy, freedom and control. When you cooperate and step out of each other's way, it's a dynamic combination. In battle you can be a pair of warring wills, fighting it out till the bitter end.

At the same time, you can be a couple of mystical magicians. Together your powers of creativity, renewal, and regeneration can build a new world. Your collisions are explosive and exciting. The product of these eruptions could be enough light and heat to launch a thousand ships. At best, you create a deep, lasting alliance of resilience and indestructibility.

Hints for Your Aries Mate

Both of you, ruled by the fiery red planet Mars, may think that combat is the cure for being frustrated and thwarted. Wrong! You know your Aries mate will argue till dawn against your scalpel-sharp criticism. There's no winning, and as your thrust gets parried, the blade gets dulled. Of course, you must be brave and heroic in the areas where your bold Aries mate wavers. Always insist that your mate be on time for appointments, follow through on commitments, see to the details of the grand plan. Remind him or her in advance; don't wait till the mistake is made so you can heap failure on Aries. That's where the arguments start. Another area is money. Hide it, bank it, keep it away from your mate's pocket where a hole is burning. A third area is flirtation. Come down hard here, even if you have to give ultimatums. Your sex life with Aries is so magnificent, she or he will not want it threatened by any foolishness.

SCORPIO—TAURUS

Here is an exciting blend of the spiritual and the material. You both appreciate what this world has to offer and love the pleasures of this earthly life. But you are opposites after all, and harmony without opposition and conflict will be impossible. You both may feel a lightning upsurge of electricity, need for change, excitement, emotional and sexual growth, and the feeling of independence. The shock of sudden crisis and reversal, the creative challenge that awakens you to life and its meaning—the power and drives of our primitive desires—these are the keys that will unlock the future for this combination.

If you are not to go to war over every last possession or descend into the depths of self-indulgence, you will have to look for values beyond simple materialism. You're both loyal, protective, and fiercely possessive. You can be staunch friends and honorable companions. Your mutual attraction is so powerful that it would take a tremendous explosion to separate you.

Finances are an integral part of your partnership. So is sex. They can destroy your relationship, or they can enhance it. It all depends on your success in developing your values.

Hints for Your Taurus Mate

You and Taurus can be opposites or zodiacal mates, depending on what you both do with the fact that you are polarized in the astrological scheme of things. You both have a lot to learn from each other. For example, you, Scorpio, must borrow the Taurus gift of patience, cooling things out before you have to placate your mate when he or she sees red. Sometimes it is you who ruffles your mate's placid exterior with criticism and demands; that's waving the red flag in front of the Bull. Your loyalty matches that of your Taurus mate, but she or he doesn't want to wait till you've separated to learn how much you care. Have more respect for the little things your mate likes by joining them. Enjoy the ease of a comfortable home, fool around with all the gadgets, fix them without complaining. Relax with wine and food, hold hands in the movies, munching popcorn, meander home, dwelling on the pleasures you've tasted instead of delivering a high-pressure lecture about tomorrow.

SCORPIO—GEMINI

This match can surge with the new life you can sense in the air on a spring day. It can also have the sting of a swarm of bees. Together you form a blend of dark intensity and joyous frivolity. Emotionally and sexually you can be a mighty exciting pair, mutually stimulating primitive passions with a light humorous approach to sex and life. This relationship will surely cover a lot of territory—from the deepest seas of emotion to the airy spheres of the mind.

At your worst, the pair of you can cook up some very strange schemes. You can be devious, plotting, or escapist with each other. You can go to great lengths to get away from each other, then go through equally elaborate efforts to get back together. Yours can be a conflict between the need for constancy and restless promiscuity.

At best, you are the perfect blend of prolific creativity and mental dexterity. You can experiment in the emotions or in the mind, joining the power to penetrate deeply and the capacity to skim the surface. Of all the combinations in the Zodiac, yours will need the greatest latitude if it is to survive. You are curious about each other, yet remain in a way strangers. Your approach to life is different. Your minds work differently. Your aims are far apart. But these differences will fascinate you with each other and, strangely enough, will show you how similar you are.

Hints for Your Gemini Mate

In this union you learn very, very slowly that your Gemini mate is as enigmatic as you are deep. He or she says things unabashed that you have feared to think. Don't get mad when your mate lets the cat out of the bag socially or with your colleagues. Praise him or her, and wait to hear what other pearls of wisdom Gemini will confide to you in private. Gemini knows a lot of things, but can't always pull them together to make an organized whole. Be a tolerant listener, fair judge, and then go ahead and nudge your mate to perform. What you come up with together can last you both a lifetime. You don't have to be afraid your criticism will wither your Gemini partner; on the contrary, it acts as a catalyst. And don't be afraid to show your possessiveness; Gemini likes someone waiting in the wings. Also, ignore your mate's flirtations; they are superficial, friendly gestures.

SCORPIO—CANCER

Feeling rules your relationship. If it's a love affair you're having, it is rich both in powerful animal desires and in your souls' need to share a spiritual union. You're an emotional pair, the feelings running from the simplest everyday moods to deep, unconscious compulsions. Sexually, you may be drawn to each other with a hunger and passion that cannot be satisfied. You are both moody jealous types, private people whose territorial instincts resent any unwanted intruder who's stalking around. You are possessive, loyal, and obsessively protective of each other, a blend of sympathy and stamina, instinct and shrewd calculation.

At worst, you fight an emotional war—living under the shadow of jealousy, revenge, and insecurity. Materialism and greed can render you cynical and alienated, narrow, clannish, and power-oriented, unwilling to open up and unable to warm up or trust.

At best, you are the defenders of life. You have a natural instinct to mate and raise children, to maintain your religious and ethical codes, and to carry on the traditions of your ancestors with dignity and integrity. Love is the overpowering ingredient that floods your being and unites your combined spirits in fertility and fruitfulness. Share these.

Hints for Your Cancer Mate

Acquisitiveness runs through this relationship, complicated by your desire to show off what you have and what you know to your Cancer mate. Those tactics might have won your lover's heart in the courtship days, but you'll earn no admiration from them in the settling period. Cancer is a healer, not a competitor or warrior. Drawn initially to your magnetism and willpower, Cancer really loves you for the frail underside of your emotions—and expects to help you reassert yourself in crisis so both of you get the benefit of your so-called regenerative powers. Cancer basically is tougher than you, a fact you'll have to respect around the threshold of home, the corridors of career, the swinging doors of society. Don't let childish greed or jealousy destroy the finest alliance you can make. Let your sexual, emotional compatibility reassure you, then follow Cancer's instincts about money and things.

SCORPIO—LEO

You connect on deep emotional levels and can understand each other well, although you will not always agree. You are both aware of passion and desire. You both manage well in crisis situations and know how to emerge victorious from battle. You are connected by feeling, look up to one another, and find comfort and security in each other.

Sexually this is a steamy match, a hot-blooded battle of drives and feelings. Though drawn to it, you cannot stand domination from each other, and your conflict may be as fierce as your passions are. At worst, you are battling for control and manipulation. Jealousy, revenge, insecurity, and pain could take hold under the wrong influences. There could be a tapping of strength, a ruthless power struggle that would be difficult to end once it had begun.

At best, this is a tender, loving match, filled with consideration and concern. You help each other through crisis, feed each other, nourish each other sexually or emotionally, and enrich each other's spirit through the benefits of your individual experiences. You are as primitive and powerful as love and death, and your blend can imbue you both with the spirit of life. As tender as the reunion between parent and child, yours is a strong union, resistant to change or invasion and gifted with the power of regeneration.

Hints for Your Leo Mate

The lustiest emotions—a will to live and a sense of survival—got you and your Leo mate together in the first place, so don't douse cold water on the relationship at the first sign of pulling apart. Your tempos are different. Respect the often flickering, dulling, hidden quality of the Leo flame. Besides, your own Scorpio currents don't always run so straight and strong. And don't panic when one of Leo's pet projects blazes like a bonfire, attracting strangers, would-be lovers, hangers-on. Leo needs the flattery; allow it. The blaze is short-lived, but if in a fury of jealousy you tamper with the fuel or the spectators, you could cause your Leo partner to think twice about your loyalty. Never dampen the Leo flame with strategies, crises, ultimatums. Allow the heat of your Leo lover to carry you smoothly onward and upward.

SCORPIO—VIRGO

You're both quick-witted and clever, the possessors of shining intellect. When you get on a subject you both love, you're a pair of eager bloodhounds, covering every square inch of a topic. You've both got sharp tongues and caustic wit. The combat between you can be deadly, for you both know how to wound the other person. You can both be possessive and manipulative, compulsive and uptight. But you can also come through for each other and save the day with advice, criticism, encouragement, and supportive trust.

Work and sex will be important to your relationship as long as you know each other. Conflicts will arise between passionate desire and emotional coldness, between wanting too much and not wanting enough. But you are generally harmonious, despite your competitiveness, fretting, and moods. Your mental and sexual union can be deep and meaningful though your contacts may be few and far between rather than constant.

Because of your association, your friendships and even your life objectives may change permanently. Your relationship can be a conspiratorial one like that of a dangerous extremist and his accomplice. You are a blend of intensity and coolness. At best your relationship resembles that of pals or cousins, sharing a powerful kinship nothing can destroy. Criticism and incisive observation are your mutual assets. Your union can reflect the marriage of artistry and artisanship, creativity and practicality.

Hints for Your Virgo Mate

This relationship works best when you treat your Virgo mate as the intellectual colleague that she or he is. Both of you are healers; your combined talents will make everything right with the world, or at least that's the way you two are supposed to see things. Both of you are fixers; enjoy splitting the tasks of identifying a problem, analyzing the problem, solving the problem. Allow even your lovemaking to be subjected to the scrutiny and analysis that Virgo dearly loves. If your mate ever tries to pretend that he or she isn't really turned on, just get sexier; don't act like you're being rejected. Sometimes the littlest things give Virgo a chill, but a rigidly icy partner is not what you want; that could happen, though, if criticism comes from you. Also avoid heavy emotional scenes from which your partner will recoil. Keeping you together is at least one project in common.

SCORPIO—LIBRA

Because of you, Libra will learn how to survive financially. Contact with you will either awaken Libra's greed or kill it. A whole new sense of values will develop over time in your Libra partner. Your ideas of control and strength affect profoundly the Libra sense of yielding to the other person.

You are drawn to Libra, but the fear of surrendering your ego will send you fleeing time and again. It is hard for you not to trust wholly, but Libra's uncertainty is often your undoing. As Libra grows in strength and self-knowledge, your decisiveness is challenged.

In a relationship with Libra, you can feel trapped or drawn irresistibly into it. Your life slowly changes, because the relationship can bring a permanent revision of everything you hold dear. So powerful is the attraction that you cannot ever imagine being separated. You may believe you are naturally connected forever.

Libra is the source of life-giving inspiration and spiritual power. For Scorpio this is the most complex relationship possible. Through this relationship you will deal with trust, forgiveness, disillusion, sacrifice, cosmic obedience, and inner regeneration.

Hints for Your Libra Mate

Try always to keep the romanticism of your courtship alive with your Libra mate. Arrange your social lives so that Libra can see you surrendering to his or her graceful charms, gay party manner, unbelievably good-looking costuming. A honeymoon quality persisting in this relationship will make it work splendidly. Don't get to nit-picking about details, decisions; never force Libra into making a decision alone. With you brooding about the future and with Libra wondering how to avoid worrying about the future, the relationship could get bogged down in false starts and stops. If you brood less, Libra will wonder less, and both of you will be able to get on with the business of everyday living. Save the weekends for the bright glitter and chatter of company that make both of you know you're the loveliest couple in town.

SCORPIO—SCORPIO

Once you two have united, you will never again be truly free. Your involvement is profoundly deep, lasting, and emotional. You both live on the horizon between light and dark, life and death. You are both capable of vengeance and jealousy, greed and lust. You have enormous cunning, and like to control your opponent from a position of utter strength.

Strangely enough, you don't often come to a fight-to-the-death struggle. You both prefer the indirect approach. More importantly, you have a certain respect and understanding for each other that lends mutual support in your conscious striving to develop your creative potentials and transform yourselves into higher beings. No matter how emotionally involved you get, you can regain control of yourselves when you need to, and bring the issues back to cold, hard business.

Your attraction to each other is compulsive, and you are joined by your extreme tastes, ambitions, and desires. You both need privacy, but without saying much you can communicate with each other on a level where most other people would be forbidden entrance. Your interest in sex is total and mutual. When you make peace and love each other, it's forever. Although your rivalries never die, you are loyal and protective, giving each other the power to be reborn through keen perception and strong love.

Hints for Your Scorpio Mate

It's amazing what you two Scorpio lovers allow with each other: experimentation, polygamy, distance, space. Any of those stances with any other mate in the Zodiac would not be labeled in such nonjudgmental terms, and would warrant venemous attack, punishing possessiveness. Now how can you keep it that way? Think about your own goals of regeneration; apply them with your Scorpio mate. You want the freedom to feel, heal, renew, recreate. Your mate should have it, too. But the decision must come from shared discussions, shared goals. If your mate is more determined than you are to live life a certain way, without your input, try to sustain the independence that gives you. If your mate is not as determined as you are, use your power to make separateness and freedom worthwhile goals—free-flowing currents joyously joining together as need and mood suit you both.

SCORPIO—SAGITTARIUS

Your passion for enjoyment draws you to Sagittarius, lifts you out of the depths, broadens your experience, and provides new opportunities for improving the character of your life. Sagittarius loves you with a compulsion that is often so confusing and overpowering that you could be the undoing of your Sagittarius mate. Although you could pose baffling questions that might exist as long as your relationship lasts, you can also be instrumental in awakening spirituality, deeper awareness, and higher consciousness in your partner.

You can deceive yourselves by fostering false hopes in each other, and together you can be a selfish pair of irresponsible children. On the other hand, you both share a healthy stamina and resilience to life's situations. You can save each other from brooding about impossibilities, for you both love pleasure, luxuries, and the joys of living. You share a taste for adventure and a desire to do something exciting, big, spectacular. You can brighten each other's horizons, raise each other's consciousness, share your intensity, and enlarge your scope.

Sagittarius can change your values and be your greatest asset. Appreciate the opportunity and reciprocate by being emotionally generous. Strive for higher consciousness to achieve greater happiness.

Hints for Your Sagittarius Mate

In this relationship don't fall into the habit of asking your Sagittarius mate to be accountable—in thought, word, or deed. Sagittarius might never admonish you, but long before the gambit becomes a habit, Sagittarius will feel trapped and want to move on. But you can always solicit your mate's opinions, beliefs. In fact, the more you encourage Sagittarius to talk, the better able she or he will be to put into perspective some of those dreamy notions. Cherish your mate's idealism; you have a large dose of it yourself. You should also help your mate bridge the gap between big ideas and reality, even if it means taking charge and shepherding a project along. Your mate won't feel you're bossy or restricting here, because, after all, you are such splendid equals in lovemaking.

SCORPIO—CAPRICORN

As you develop a long-term relationship based on mutual respect you will be a source of strength to each other. Yours is a union of intensity and stability. Sexually this can be a powerful match, for your involvement is anything but light. You both share a need for strong ties, and the depth of your relationship will always show that. Games of power and control may be irresistible for you both, since the two of you are strong-willed cautious types who like to feel you are indispensable to your partner. You both need acceptance and want to be loved, honored, and obeyed. When you go to war, the war can last a long time. Neither of you is a total forgiver and forgetter, and you don't trust each other easily.

You are a no-nonsense combination of sexual magnetism and career drive, for you blend an otherworldly creativity with hardheaded ambition. Sometimes you are more successful apart than together. You are apt to be better friends than lovers.

Through loyalty and practical approaches to your problems, your relationship is sure to grow and deepen, no matter how long it takes. And it will take time, for

you are both hard to know. You are both able, coura-
geous people. No struggle is too great for you both to
undertake. You both love to emerge unscathed from the
problems of life, and the older you get the tougher you
get. Maturity will be of great benefit to your association.

Hints for Your Capricorn Mate

No matter what your rank or privilege is relative to
your Capricorn mate, you are undeniably the authority
in the emotion department. Capricorn, unlike some zodiacal types, won't mind if you give intense instruction
in this area. After all, you're turning Capricorn on,
something that is hard for him or her to do on their own
behalf. Yes, Capricorn needs an authority figure to sponsor an open, lusty sexuality. Here, too, you can be the
grand master. Concentrate on these areas to develop
your relationship to its fullest. You won't have much
cause for brooding or discord in other areas. Capricorn,
like you, has a strong will, a commitment to problem
solving, and a huge desire to get on with life and get the
most out of it. But if you need to play the subordinate
somewhere, let Capricorn teach you how to make your
creativity work for you.

SCORPIO—AQUARIUS

Diplomacy, compromise, and love of justice are key solutions to the dilemma of attachment and freedom that
you two will face. Whatever conflicts arise between togetherness and separateness can shatter your dreams of
peace. But facing the storms can bring you both to a
new and exciting understanding of yourselves as individuals and in relation to each other. You are both looking for security with independence. Yet you both may
find it hard to make total and long-lasting commitments. It is very difficult for you both to relax and let

yourselves be free. Yet when you become possessive, you fear each other.

Your conflicts are between the intimate one-to-one relationships of your forebears and the free-style open scenes of experimentation. You struggle between a need for deep sexual involvements and a need for open non-sexual contacts with friends and fellow human beings in a spirit of community and harmony. Your relationship can vary from tenderness, intensity, nourishment, and growth to abrupt coldness, separation, and a peculiar lack of care and feeling.

You can have a long-lasting relationship provided you don't get too bossy and possessive and provided you don't leave your partner in the lurch to show your independence. Some rules are made to be broken. Mature individuals who love each other will have the respect and concern of their partners without demanding them. When your partner trusts you, you will have your security and freedom, too.

Hints for Your Aquarius Mate

You two can have a lot of fun talking about the brave new world while you're both heroically tending to the miserable tasks of this one. At the very least, you can document your Aquarius mate's suspicions that all is not well by delivering an ongoing, tragically personal account of the inequities and perils of life. And you are a sympathetic listener when Aquarius ingeniously describes a new design for living. Of course, all the while both of you are washing dishes, watering plants, changing the kitty litter, tripping back and forth to the laundry, sorting monthly bills. Aren't you? These little responsibilities are not very romantic, but they keep your house together and give you both time and space to dwell on the bigger issues and to mentally solve them. Let your Aquarius mate be your intellectual hero. For him or her, you are the victor in love and sex.

SCORPIO—PISCES

When you fall in love with Pisces, there is always romance, passion, confusion, indecision, disappointment, and a sweet but maddening intoxication. Together you can create a channel for mutual desires. And you both flow into a sea of emotion, swept away by love, sex, and mystery. Pisces responds to the masterful drive of Scorpio. Scorpio cuts through the Pisces indecision like a scalpel. Your purifying thrust acts like a strong conscience, healing and strengthening the Pisces mind.

Of all the combinations of zodiacal signs, yours has the most potential for effecting changes in each other's lives for good or ill. At worst you are obsessed and driven, plaguing yourselves and each other with a mixture of cruelty, self-indulgence, and escapism, addicted to pleasures and the drama of emotional conflict and personal pain, trapped in an endless cycle of attraction and repulsion.

The explosive energy you as a Scorpio feel is greatly different from the search your Pisces undertakes. Pisces is searching for self-knowledge through meditation, travel, learning, and education. Your paths may be different until you converge and meet at a point of no return.

At best, your relationship can take on mythic proportions. It can become a love affair with a sense of mission or greater purpose. Together you are the union of the selfless servant and the healer. You can break free from social rules, emotional limitations, and earthly obstacles. Together you can perform, create, enjoy, make love in an eternal union of the mind, body, and spirit.

Hints for Your Pisces Mates

Just because you both are water signs doesn't mean that you can safely inhabit the same niche without a lot of defensive maneuvering. Like the scorpion which is your symbol, you may lurk at water's edge to sting your Pisces partner as he or she glides by. And your partner, double fish like the Pisces symbol, may swim in two totally opposite directions to get away from you. The best adaptation for this relationship is for each of you to keep some parts of your lives separate and distinct. Make a contract disallowing complaints and criticism about the other's territory. Perhaps for the habitats you do share there should also be stringent rules about who does what when, such as household chores, entertaining, use of the computer, typewriter, telephone. You'll interact swimmingly, though, in the realms of sex and emotion.

SCORPIO:
YOUR PROGRESSED SUN

WHAT IS YOUR NEW SIGN

Your birth sign, or Sun sign, is the central core of your whole personality. It symbolizes everything you try to do and be. It is your main streak, your major source of power, vitality, and life. But as you live you learn, and as you learn you progress. The element in your horoscope that measures your progress is called the Progressed Sun. It is the symbol of your growth on Earth, and represents new threads that run through your life. The Progressed Sun measures big changes, turning points, and major decisions. It will often describe the path you are taking toward the fulfillment of your desires.

Below you will find brief descriptions of the Progressed Sun in three signs. According to the table on page 43, find out about your Progressed Sun and see how and where you fit into the cosmic scheme. Each period lasts about 30 years, so watch and see how dramatic these changes turn out to be.

If Your Sun Is Progressing Into—

SAGITTARIUS, look up, for your life will be much brighter from now on. You will find great encouragement for living, for sports, for travel. Your power of learning will increase. Religion, politics, philosophy, and higher learning will enter your life at this time. Though your aims may be unrealistic and overexpansive, you will be buoyed up by good cheer.

CAPRICORN, you will grow more serious during this period. Plans that are unrealistic will come to no good end. You will need to add structure to your life, confront your limitations, and examine the boundaries that govern your particular life circumstances. You'll have to start working harder to get what you want. Success will be yours during this period as long as you climb toward it.

AQUARIUS, you'll be wanting freedom from the restrictions of the past years. You will want to break new territory, throw off limitations, start fresh, and experiment with new things and new people. You will have contact with groups, societies, and friends. It is a time for advancements as you put past reversals behind you and into perspective.

HOW TO USE THE TABLE

Look for your birthday in the table on the facing page. Then under the appropriate column, find out approximately when your Progressed Sun will lead you to a new sign. From that point on, for 30 years, the thread of your life will run through that sign. Read the definitions on the preceding pages and see exactly how that life thread will develop.

For example, if your birthday is October 30, your Progressed Sun will enter Sagittarius around your 24th birthday and will travel through Sagittarius until you are 54 years old. Your Progressed Sun will then move into Capricorn. Reading the definitions of Sagittarius and Capricorn will tell you much about your major involvements and interests during those years.

YOUR PROGRESSED SUN

If your birthday falls on:	start looking at SAGITTARIUS at age	start looking at CAPRICORN at age	start looking at AQUARIUS at age
Oct. 23–24	.30	.60	.90
25	.29	.59	.89
26	.28	.58	.88
27	.27	.57	.87
28	.26	.56	.86
29	.25	.55	.85
30	.24	.54	.84
31	.23	.53	.83
November 1	.22	.52	.82
2	.21	.51	.81
3	.20	.50	.80
4	.19	.49	.79
5	.18	.48	.78
6	.17	.47	.77
7	.16	.46	.76
8	.15	.45	.75
9	.14	.44	.74
10	.13	.43	.73
11	.12	.42	.72
12	.11	.41	.71
13	.10	.40	.70
14	.9	.39	.69
15	.8	.38	.68
16	.7	.37	.67
17	.6	.36	.66
18	.5	.35	.65
19	.4	.34	.64
20	.3	.33	.63
21	.2	.32	.62
22	.1	.31	.61

SCORPIO BIRTHDAYS

Oct. 23   Sarah Bernhardt, Johnny Carson
Oct. 24   Moss Hart, Jimmy Dawkins
Oct. 25   Pablo Picasso, Helen Reddy
Oct. 26   Mahalia Jackson, Margaret Leighton
Oct. 27   Teddy Roosevelt, Ruby Dee, Sylvia Plath
Oct. 28   Elsa Lancaster, Jonas Salk
Oct. 29   Fanny Brice, Bill Mauldin
Oct. 30   Charles Atlas, Grace Slick
Oct. 31   Dale Evans, Ethel Waters
Nov. 1   Stephen Crane, Victoria de Los Ángeles
Nov. 2   Daniel Boone, Burt Lancaster
Nov. 3   Andre Malraux
Nov. 4   Will Rogers, Walter Cronkite
Nov. 5   Roy Rogers, Art Garfunkel
Nov. 6   James Jones, Mike Nichols
Nov. 7   Marie Curie, Joni Mitchell
Nov. 8   Katharine Hepburn, Margaret Mitchell
Nov. 9   Hedy Lamarr, Marie Dressler
Nov. 10   Martin Luther, Richard Burton
Nov. 11   Abigal Adams, Kurt Vonnegut
Nov. 12   Grace Kelly, Elizabeth Stanton
Nov. 13   Robert Louis Stevenson, Eugene Ionesco
Nov. 14   Jawaharlal Nehru, Marya Mannes
Nov. 15   Marianne Moore, Georgia O'Keefe
Nov. 16   Burgess Meredith
Nov. 17   Rock Hudson
Nov. 18   Eugene Ormandy, Dorothy Dix
Nov. 19   Indira Gandhi, Dick Cavett
Nov. 20   Bobby Kennedy, Estelle Parsons
Nov. 21   Voltaire, Goldie Hawn, Marlo Thomas
Nov. 22   George Eliot, Geraldine Page,
             Billie Jean King

CAN ASTROLOGY PREDICT THE FUTURE?

Can astrology really peer into the future? By studying the planets and the stars is it possible to look years ahead and make predictions for our lives? How can we draw the line between ignorant superstition and cosmic mystery? We live in a very civilized world, to be sure. We consider ourselves modern, enlightened individuals. Yet few of us can resist the temptation to take a peek at the future when we think it's possible. Why? What is the basis of such universal curiosity?

The answer is simple. Astrology works, and you don't have to be a magician to find that out. We certainly can't prove astrology simply by taking a look at the astonishing number of people who believe in it, but such figures do make us wonder what lies behind such widespread popularity. Everywhere in the world hundreds of thousands of serious, intelligent people are charting, studying, and interpreting the positions of the planets and stars every day. Every facet of the media dispenses daily astrological bulletins to millions of curious seekers. In Eastern countries, the source of many wisdoms handed down to us from antiquity, astrology still has a vital place. Why? Surrounded as we are by sophisticated scientific method, how does astrology, with all its bizarre symbolism and mysterious meaning, survive so magnificently? The answer remains the same. It works.

Nobody knows exactly where astrological knowledge came from. We have references to it dating back to the dawn of human history. Wherever there was a stirring of human consciousness, people began to observe the natural cycles and rhythms that sustained their life. The diversity of human behavior must have been evident even to the first students of consciousness. Yet the basic similarity between members of the human family must have led to the search for some common source, some greater point of origin somehow linked to the heavenly bodies ruling our sense of life and time. The ancient world of Mesopotamia, Chaldea, and Egypt was a highly developed center of astronomical observation and astrological interpretation of heavenly phenomena and their resultant effects on human life.

Amid the seeming chaos of a mysterious unknown universe, people from earliest times sought to classify, define, and organize the world around them. Order: that's what the human mind has always striven to maintain in an unceasing battle with its natural counterpart, chaos, or entropy. We build cities, countries, and empires, subjugating nature to a point of near defeat, and then ... civilization collapses, empires fall, and cities crumble. Nature reclaims the wilderness. Shelly's poem *Ozymandias* is a hymn to the battle between order and chaos. The narrator tells us about a statue, broken, shattered, and half-sunk somewhere in the middle of a distant desert. The inscription reads: "Look on my works, ye mighty, and despair." And then we are told: "Nothing beside remains. Round the decay of that colossal wreck, boundless and bare, the lone and level sands stretch far away."

People always feared the entropy that seemed to lurk in nature. So we found permanence and constancy in the regular movements of the Sun, Moon, and planets and in the positions of the stars. Traditions sprang up from observations of the seasons and crops. Relationships were noted between phenomena in nature and the configurations of the heavenly bodies. This "synchronicity," as it was later called by Carl Jung, extended to thought, mood, and behavior, and as such developed the astrological archetypes handed down to us today.

Astrology, a regal science of the stars in the old days, was made available to the king, who was informed of impending events in the heavens, translated of course to their earthly meanings by trusted astrologers. True, astrological knowledge in its infant stages was rudimentary and beset with many superstitions and false premises. But those same dangers exist today in any investigation of occult or mystical subjects. In the East, reverence for astrology is part of religion. Astrologer-astronomers have held respected positions in government and have taken part in advisory councils on many momentous issues. The duties of the court astrologer, whose office was one of the most important in the land, were clearly defined, as early records show.

Here in our sleek Western world, astrology glimmers on, perhaps more brilliantly than ever. With all of our technological wonders and complex urbanized environments, we look to astrology even now to cut through artificiality, dehumanization, and all the materialism of contemporary life, while we gather precious information that helps us live in that material world. Astrology helps us restore balance and get in step with our own rhythms and the rhythms of nature.

Intelligent investigation of astrology (or the practical application of it) need not mean blind acceptance. We only need to see it working, see our own lives confirming its principles every day, in order to accept and understand it more. To understand ourselves is to know ourselves and to know all. This book can help you to do that—to understand yourself and through understanding develop your own resources and potentials as a rich human being.

YOUR PLACE AMONG THE STARS

Humanity finds itself at the center of a vast personal universe that extends infinitely outward in all directions. In that sense each is a kind of star radiating, as our Sun does, to all bodies everywhere. These vibrations, whether loving, helpful, or destructive, extend outward and generate a kind of "atmosphere" in which woman and man move. The way we relate to everything around us—our joy or our sorrow—becomes a living part of us. Our loved ones and our enemies become the objects of our projected radiations, for better or worse. Our bodies and faces reflect thoughts and emotions much the way light from the Sun reflects the massive reactions occurring deep within its interior. This energy and light reach all who enter its sphere of influence.

Our own personal radiations are just as potent in their own way, really. The reactions that go on deep within us profoundly affect our way of thinking and acting. Our feelings of joy or satisfaction, frustration or anger, must eventually find an outlet. Otherwise we experience the psychological or physiological repercussions of repression. If we can't have a good cry, tell someone our troubles, or express love, we soon feel very bad indeed.

As far as our physical selves are concerned, there is a direct relationship between our outer lives, inner reactions and actions, and the effects on our physical body. We all know the feeling of being startled by the sudden ring of a telephone, or the simple frustration of missing a bus. In fact, our minds and bodies are constantly reacting to outside forces. At the same time we, too, are generating actions that will cause a reaction in someone else. You may suddenly decide to phone a friend. If you are a bus driver you might speed along on your way and leave behind an angry would-be passenger. Whatever the case, mind and body are in close communication and they both reflect each other's condition. Next time you're really angry take a good long look in the mirror!

In terms of human evolution, our ability to understand, control, and ultimately change ourselves will naturally affect all of our outside relationships. Astrology is invaluable to helping us comprehend our inner selves. It is a useful tool in helping us retain our integrity, while cooperating with and living in a world full of other human beings.

Let's go back to our original question: Can astrology predict the future? To know that, we must come to an understanding of what the future is.

In simplest terms the future is the natural next step to the present, just as the present is a natural progression from the past. Although our minds can move from one to the other, there is a thread of continuity between past, present, and future that joins them together in a coherent sequence. If you are reading this book at this moment, it is the result of a real conscious choice you made in the recent past. That is, you chose to find out what was on these pages, picked up the book, and opened it. Because of this choice you may know yourself better in the future. It's as simple as that.

Knowing ourselves is the key to being able to predict and understand our own future. To learn from past experiences, choices, and actions is to fully grasp the present. Coming to grips with the present is to be master of the future.

"Know thyself" is a motto that takes us back to the philosophers of ancient Greece. Mystery religions and cults of initiation throughout the ancient world, schools of mystical discipline, yoga and mental expansion have always been guardians of this one sacred phrase. Know thyself. Of course, that's easy to say. But how do you go about it when there are so many conflicts in our lives and different parts of our personalities? How do we know when we are really "being ourselves" and not merely being influenced by the things we read or see on television, or by the people around us? How can we differentiate the various parts of our character and still remain whole?

There are many methods of classifying human beings into types. Body shapes, muscular types, blood types, and genetic types are only a few. Psychology has its own ways of classifying human beings according to their behavior. Anthropology studies human evolution as the body-mind response to environment. Biology watches physical development and adaptations in body structure. These fields provide valuable information about human beings and the ways they survive, grow, and change in their search for their place in eternity. Yet these branches of science have been separate and fragmented. Their contribution has been to provide theories and data, yes, but no lasting solutions to the human problems that have existed since the first two creatures realized they had two separate identities.

It's often difficult to classify yourself according to these different schemes. It's not easy to be objective about yourself. Some things are hard to face; others are hard to see. The different perspectives afforded to us by studying the human organism from all these different disciplines may seem contradictory when they are all really trying to integrate humankind into the whole of the cosmic scheme.

Astrology can help these disciplines unite to seek a broader and deeper approach to universal human issues. Astrology's point of view is vast. It transcends racial, ethnic, genetic, environmental, and even historical criteria, yet somehow includes them all. Astrology embraces the totality of human experience, then sets about to examine the relationships that are created within that experience.

We don't simply say, "The planets cause this or that." Rather than merely isolating cause or effect, astrology has unified the ideas of cause and effect. Concepts of past, present, and future merge and become, as we shall see a little later on, like stepping-stones across the great stream of mind. Observations of people and the environment have developed the astrological principles of planetary "influence," but it must be remembered that if there is actual influence, it is mutual. As the planets influence us, so we influence them, for we are forever joined to all past and future motion of the heavenly bodies. This is the foundation of astrology as it has been built up over the centuries.

ORDER VS. CHAOS

But is it all written in the stars? Is it destined that empires should thrive and flourish, kings reign, lovers love, and then . . . decay, ruin, and natural disintegration hold sway? Have we anything to do with determining the cycles of order and chaos? The art of the true astrologer depends on his ability to uncover new information, place it upon the grid of data already collected, and then interpret what he sees as accurate probability in human existence. There may be a paradox here. If we can predict that birds will fly south, could we not, with enough time and samples for observation, determine their ultimate fate when they arrive in the south?

The paradox is that there is no paradox at all. Order and chaos exist together simultaneously in one observable universe. At some remote point in time and space the Earth was formed, and for one reason or another, life appeared here. Whether the appearance of life on planets is a usual phenomenon or an unrepeated accident we can only speculate at this moment. But our

Earth and all living things upon its surface conform to certain laws of physical materiality that our observations have led us to write down and contemplate. All creatures, from the one-celled ameba to a man hurrying home at rush hour, have some basic traits in common. Life in its organization goes from the simple to the complex with a perfection and order that is both awesome and inspiring. If there were no order to our physical world, an apple could turn into a worm and cows could be butterflies.

But the world is an integrated whole, unified with every other part of creation. When nature does take an unexpected turn, we call that a mutation. This is the exciting card in the program of living experience that tells us not everything is written at all. Spontaneity is real. Change is real. Freedom from the expected norm is real. We have seen in nature that only those mutations that can adapt to changes in their environment and continue reproducing themselves will survive. But possibilities are open for sudden transformation, and that keeps the whole world growing.

FREE CHOICE AND
THE VALUE OF PREDICTIONS

Now it's time to turn our attention to the matter of predictions. That was our original question after all: Can astrology peer into the future? Well, astrological prognostication is an awe-inspiring art and requires deep philosophical consideration before it is to be undertaken. Not only are there many grids that must be laid one upon the other before such predictions can be made, but there are ethical issues that plague every student of the stars. How much can you really see? How much should you tell? What is the difference between revealing valuable data and disclosing negative or harmful programing?

If an astrologer tells you only the good things, you'll have little confidence in the analysis when you are passing through crisis. On the other hand, if the astrologer is a prophet of doom who can see nothing but the dark clouds on the horizon, you will eventually have to reject astrology because you will come to associate it with the bad luck in your life.

Astrology itself is beyond any practitioner's capacity to grasp it all. Unrealistic utopianism or gloomy determinism reflect not the truth of astrology but the truth of the astrologer interpreting what he sees. In order to solve problems and make accurate predictions, you have to be *able* to look on the dark side of things without dwelling there. You have to be able to take a look at all the possibilities, all the possible meanings of a certain planetary influence without jumping to premature conclusions. Objective scanning and assessment take much practice and great skill.

No matter how skilled the astrologer is, he cannot assume the responsibility for your life. Only you can take that responsibility as your life unfolds. In a way, the predictions of this book are glancing ahead up the road, much the way a road map can indicate turns up ahead this way or that. You, however, are still driving the car.

What, then, is a horoscope? If it is a picture of you at your moment of birth, are you then frozen forever in time and space, unable to budge or deviate from the harsh, unyielding declarations of the stars? Not at all.

The universe is always in motion. Each moment follows the moment before it. As the present is the result of all past choices and action, so the future is the result of today's choices. But if we can go to a planetary calendar and see where planets will be located two years from now, then how can individual free choice exist? This is a question that has haunted authors and philosophers since the first thinkers recorded their thoughts. In the end, of course, we must all reason things out for ourselves and come to our own conclusions. It is easy to be impressed or influenced by people who seem to know a lot more than we do, but in reality we must all find codes of beliefs with which we are the most comfortable.

But if we can stretch our imaginations up, up above the line of time as it exists from one point to another, we can almost see past, present, and future, all together. We can almost feel this vibrant thread of creative free choice that pushes forward at every moment, actually causing the future to happen! Free will, that force that changes the entire course of a stream, exists within the stream of mind itself—the collective mind, or intelligence, of humanity. Past, present, and future are mere stepping-stones across that great current.

Our lives continue a thread of an intelligent mind that existed before we were born and will exist after we die. It is like an endless relay race. At birth we pick up a torch and carry it, lighting the way with that miraculous light of consciousness of immortality. Then we pass it on to others when we die. What we call the *unconscious* may be part of this great stream of mind, which learns and shares experiences with everything that has ever lived or will ever live on this world or any other.

Yet we all come to Earth with different family circumstances, backgrounds, and characteristics. We all come to life with different planetary configurations. Indeed each person *is* different, yet we are all the same. We have different tasks or responsibilities or lifestyles, but underneath we share a common current—the powerful stream of human intelligence. Each of us has different sets of circumstances to deal with because of the choices he or she has made in the past. We all possess different assets and have different resources to fall back on, weaknesses to strengthen, and sides of our nature to transform. We are all what we are now because of what we were before. The present is the sum of the past. And we will be what we will be in the future because of what we are now.

It is foolish to pretend that there are no specific boundaries or limitations to any of our particular lives. Family background, racial, cultural, or religious indoctrinations, physical characteristics, these are all inescapable facts of our being that must be incorporated and accepted into our maturing mind. But each person possesses the capacity for breakthrough, forgiveness, and total transformation. It has taken millions of years since people first began to walk upright. We cannot expect an overnight evolution to take place. There are many things about our personalities that are very much like our parents. Sometimes that thought makes us uncomfortable, but it's true.

It's also true that we are not our parents. You are *you*, just you, and nobody else but you. That's one of the wondrous aspects of astrology. The levels on which each planetary configuration works out will vary from individual to individual. Often an aspect of selfishness will be manifested in one person, yet in another it may appear as sacrifice and kindness.

Development is inevitable in human consciousness. But the direction of that development is not. As plants will bend toward the light as they grow, so there is the possibility for the human mind to grow toward the light of integrity and truth. The Age of Aquarius that everyone is talking about must first take place within each human's mind and heart. An era of peace, freedom, and community cannot be legislated by any government, no matter how liberal. It has to be a spontaneous flow of human spirit and fellowship. It will be a magnificent dawning on the globe of consciousness that reflects the joy of the human heart to be part of the great stream of intelligence and love. It must be generated by an enlightened, realistic humanity. There's no law that can put it into effect, no magic potion to drink that will make it all come true. It will be the result of all people's efforts to assume their personal and social responsibilities and to carve out a new destiny for humankind.

As you read the predictions in this book, bear in mind that they have been calculated by means of planetary positions for whole groups of people. Thus their value lies in your ability to coordinate what you read with the nature of your life's circumstances at the present time. You have seen how many complex relationships must be analyzed in individual horoscopes before sensible accurate conclusions can be drawn. No matter what the indications, a person has his or her own life, own intelligence, basic native strength that must ultimately be the source of action and purpose. When you are living truthfully and in harmony with what you know is right, there are no forces, threats, or obstacles that can defeat you.

With these predictions, read the overall pattern and see how rhythms begin to emerge. They are not caused by remote alien forces, millions of miles out in space.

You and the planets are one. What you do, they do. What they do, you do. But can you change their course? No, but you cannot change many of your basic characteristics either. Still, within that already existing framework, you are the master. You can still differentiate between what is right for you and what is not. You can seize opportunities and act on them, you can create beauty and seek love.

The purpose of looking ahead is not to scare yourself. Look ahead to enlarge your perspective, enhance your overall view of the life *you* are developing. Difficult periods cause stress certainly, but at the same time they give you the chance to reassess your condition, restate and redefine exactly what is important to you, so you can cherish your life more. Joyous periods should be lived to the fullest with the happiness and exuberance that each person richly deserves.

YOUR HOROSCOPE AND THE ZODIAC

It's possible that in your own body, as you read this passage, there exist atoms as old as time itself. You could well be the proud possessor of some carbon and hydrogen (two necessary elements in the development of life) that came into being in the heart of a star billions and billions of years ago. That star could have exploded and cast its matter far into space. This matter could have formed another star, and then another, until finally our Sun was born. From the Sun's nuclear reactions came the material that later formed the planets—and maybe some of that primeval carbon or hydrogen. That material could have become part of the Earth, part of an early ocean, even early life. These same atoms could well have been carried down to the present day, to this very moment as you read this book. It's really quite possible. You can see how everything is linked to everything else. Our Earth now exists in a gigantic universe that showers it constantly with rays and invisible particles. You are the point into which all these energies and influences have been focused. You are the prism through which all the light of outer space is being refracted. You are literally a reflection of all the planets and stars.

Your horoscope is a picture of the sky at the moment of your birth. It's like a gigantic snapshot of the positions of the planets and stars, taken from Earth. Of course, the planets never stop moving around the Sun even for the briefest moment, and you represent that motion as it was occurring at the exact hour of your birth at the precise location on the Earth where you were born.

When an astrologer is going to read your chart, he or she asks you for the month, day, and year of your birth. She also needs the exact time and place. With this information he sets about consulting various charts and tables in his calculation of the specific positions of the Sun, Moon, and stars, relative to your birthplace when you came to Earth. Then he or she locates them by means of the *Zodiac*.

The Zodiac is a group of stars, centered against the Sun's apparent path around the Earth, and these star groups are divided into twelve equal segments, or *signs*. What we are actually dividing up is the Earth's path around the Sun. But from our point of view here on Earth, it seems as if the Sun is making a great circle around our planet in the sky, so we say it's the Sun's apparent path. This twelvefold division, the Zodiac, is like a mammoth address system for any body in the sky. At any given moment, the planets can all be located at a specific point along this path.

Now where are you in this system? First you look to your *Sun sign*—the section of the Zodiac that the Sun occupied when you were born. A great part of your character, in fact the central thread of your whole being, is described by your Sun sign. Each sign of the Zodiac has certain basic traits associated with it. Since the Sun remains in each sign for about thirty days, that divides the population into twelve major character types. Of course, not everybody born the same month will have the same character, but you'll be amazed at how many fundamental traits you share with your astrological cousins of the same birth sign, no matter how many environmental differences you boast.

The dates on which the Sun sign changes will vary from year to year. That is why some people born near the *cusp*, or edge, of a sign have difficulty determining their true birth sign without the aid of an astrologer who can plot precisely the Sun's apparent motion (the Earth's motion) for any given year. But to help you find your true Sun sign, a Table of Cusp Dates for the years 1900 to 2010 is provided for you on page 17.

Here are the twelve signs of the Zodiac as western astrology has recorded them. Listed also are the symbols associated with them and the *approximate* dates when the Sun enters and exits each sign for the year 2007.

Aries	Ram	March 20–April 20
Taurus	Bull	April 20–May 21
Gemini	Twins	May 21–June 21
Cancer	Crab	June 21–July 23
Leo	Lion	July 23–August 23
Virgo	Virgin	August 23–September 23
Libra	Scales	September 23–October 23
Scorpio	Scorpion	October 23–November 22
Sagittarius	Archer	November 22–December 22
Capricorn	Sea Goat	December 22–January 20
Aquarius	Water Bearer	January 20–February 18
Pisces	Fish	February 18–March 20

In a horoscope the *Rising sign*, or Ascendant, is often considered to be as important as the Sun sign. In a later chapter (see pages 82–84) the Rising sign is discussed in detail. But to help you determine your own Rising sign, a Table of Rising Signs is provided for you on pages 20–21.

THE SIGNS OF THE ZODIAC

The signs of the Zodiac are an ingenious and complex summary of human behavioral and physical types, handed down from generation to generation through the bodies of all people in their hereditary material and through their minds. On the following pages you will find brief descriptions of all twelve signs in their highest and most ideal expression.

ARIES
The Sign of the Ram

Aries is the first sign of the Zodiac, and marks the beginning of springtime and the birth of the year. In spring the Earth begins its ascent upward and tips its North Pole toward the Sun. During this time the life-giving force of the Sun streams toward Earth, bathing our planet with the kiss of warmth and life. Plants start growing. Life wakes up. No more waiting. No more patience. The message has come from the Sun: Time to live!

Aries is the sign of the Self and is the crusade for the right of an individual to live in unimpeachable freedom. It represents the supremacy of the human will over all obstacles, limitations, and threats. In Aries there is unlimited energy, optimism, and daring, for it is the pioneer in search of a new world. It is the story of success and renewal, championship, and victory. It is the living spirit of resilience and the power to be yourself, free from all restrictions and conditioning. There is no pattern you *have* to repeat, nobody's rule you *have* to follow.

Confidence and positive action are born in Aries, with little thought or fear of the past. Life is as magic as sunrise, with all the creative potential ahead of you for a new day. Activity, energy, and adventure characterize this sign. In this sector of the Zodiac there is amazing strength, forthrightness, honesty, and a stubborn refusal to accept defeat. The Aries nature is forgiving, persuasive, masterful, and decisive.

In short, Aries is the magic spark of life and being, the source of all initiative, courage, independence, and self-esteem.

TAURUS
The Sign of the Bull

Taurus is wealth. It is not just money, property, and the richness of material possessions, but also a wealth of the spirit. Taurus rules everything in the visible world we see, touch, hear, smell, taste—the Earth, sea, and sky—everything we normally consider "real." It is the sign of economy and reserve, for it is a mixture of thrift and luxury, generosity and practicality. It is a blend of the spiritual and material, for the fertility of the sign is unlimited, and in this sense it is the mystical bank of life. Yet it must hold the fruit of its efforts in its hands and seeks to realize its fantasy-rich imagination with tangible rewards.

Loyalty and endurance make this sign perhaps the most stable of all. We can lean on Taurus, count on it, and it makes our earthly lives comfortable, safe, pleasurable. It is warm, sensitive, loving, and capable of magnificent, joyful sensations. It is conservative and pragmatic, with a need to be sure of each step forward. It is the capacity to plan around eventualities without living in the future. Steadfast and constant, this is a sturdy combination of ruggedness and beauty, gentleness and unshakability of purpose. It is the point at which we join body and soul. Unselfish friend and loyal companion, Taurus is profoundly noble and openly humanitarian. Tenacity and concentration slow the energy down to bring certain long-lasting rewards.

Taurus is a fertile resource and rich ground to grow in, and we all need it for our ideas and plans to flourish. It is the uncut diamond, symbolizing rich, raw tastes and a deep need for satisfaction, refinement, and completion.

GEMINI
The Sign of the Twins

Gemini is the sign of mental brilliance. Communication is developed to a high degree of fluidity, rapidity, fluency. It is the chance for expressing ideas and relaying information from one place to another. Charming, debonair, and lighthearted, it is a symbol of universal interest and eternal curiosity. The mind is quick and advanced, with a lightning-like ability to assimilate data.

It is the successful manipulation of verbal or visual language and the capacity to meet all events with objectivity and intelligence. It is light, quick wit, with a comic satiric twist. Gemini is the sign of writing or speaking.

Gemini is the willingness to try anything once, a need to wander and explore, the quick shifting of moods and attitudes being a basic characteristic that indicates a need for change. Versatility is the remarkable Gemini attribute. It is the capacity to investigate, perform, and relate over great areas for short periods of time and thus to connect all areas. It is mastery of design and perception, the power to conceptualize and create by putting elements together—people, colors, patterns. It is the reporter's mind, plus a brilliant ability to see things in objective, colorful arrangement. Strength lies in constant refreshment of outlook and joyful participation in all aspects of life.

Gemini is involvement with neighbors, family and relatives, telephones, arteries of news and communication—anything that enhances the human capacity for communication and self-expression. It is active, positive, and energetic, with an insatiable hunger for human interchange. Through Gemini bright and dark sides of personality merge and the mind has wings. As it flies it reflects the light of a boundless shining intellect. It is the development of varied talents from recognition of the duality of self.

Gemini is geared toward enjoying life to the fullest by finding, above all else, a means of expressing the inner self to the outside world.

CANCER
The Sign of the Crab

Cancer is the special relationship to home and involvement with the family unit. Maintaining harmony in the domestic sphere or improving conditions there is a major characteristic in this sector of the Zodiac. Cancer is attachment between two beings vibrating in sympathy with one another.

It is the comfort of a loving embrace, a tender generosity. Cancer is the place of shelter whenever there are lost or hungry souls in the night. Through Cancer we are fed, protected, comforted, and soothed. When the coldness of the world threatens, Cancer is there with gentle understanding. It is protection and understated loyalty, a medium of rich, living feeling that is both psychic and mystical. Highly intuitive, Cancer has knowledge that other signs do not possess. It is the wisdom of the soul.

It prefers the quiet contentment of the home and hearth to the busy search for earthly success and civilized pleasures. Still, there is a respect for worldly knowledge. Celebration of life comes through food. The sign is the muted light of warmth, security, and gladness, and its presence means nourishment. It rules fertility and the instinct to populate and raise young. It is growth of the soul. It is the ebb and flow of all our tides of feeling, involvements, habits, and customs.

Through Cancer is reflected the inner condition of all human beings, and therein lies the seed of knowledge out of which the soul will grow.

LEO
The Sign of the Lion

Leo is love. It represents the warmth, strength, and regeneration we feel through love. It is the radiance of life-giving light and the center of all attention and activity. It is passion, romance, adventure, and games. Pleasure, amusement, fun, and entertainment are all part of

Leo. Based on the capacity for creative feeling and the desire to express love, Leo is the premier sign. It represents the unlimited outpouring of all that is warm and positive.

It is loyalty, dignity, responsibility, and command. Pride and nobility belong to Leo, and the dashing image of the knight in shining armor, of the hero, is part of Leo. It is a sense of high honor and kingly generosity born out of deep, noble love. It is the excitement of the sportsman, with all the unbeatable flair and style of success. It is a strong, unyielding will and true sense of personal justice, a respect for human freedom, and an enlightened awareness of people's needs.

Leo is involvement in the Self's awareness of personal talents and the desire and need to express them. At best it is forthrightness, courage and efficiency, authority and dignity, showmanship, and a talent for organization. Dependable and ardent, the Lion is characterized by individuality, positivism, and integrity.

It is the embodiment of human maturity, the effective individual in society, a virile creative force able to take chances and win. It is the love of laughter and the joy of making others happy. Decisive and enthusiastic, the Lion is the creative producer of the Zodiac It is the potential to light the way for others.

VIRGO
The Sign of the Virgin

Virgo is the sign of work and service. It is the symbol of the farmer at harvest time, and represents tireless efforts for the benefit of humanity, the joy of bringing the fruits of the Earth to the table of mankind. Celebration through work is the characteristic of this sign.

Sincerity, zeal, discipline, and devotion mark the sign of the Virgin.

The key word is purity, and in Virgo lies a potential for unlimited self-mastery. Virgo is the embodiment of perfected skill and refined talent. The thread of work is woven into the entire life of Virgo. All creativity is poured into streamlining a job, classifying a system, eradicating unnecessary elements of pure analysis. The true Virgo genius is found in separating the wheat from the chaff.

Spartan simplicity characterizes this sign, and Virgo battles the war between order and disorder. The need to arrange, assimilate, and categorize is great; it is the symbol of the diagnostician, the nurse, and the healer. Criticism and analysis describe this sign—pure, incisive wisdom and a shy appreciation of life's joys. All is devoted to the attainment of perfection and the ideal of self-mastery.

Virgo is the sign of health and represents the physical body as a functioning symbol of the mental and spiritual planes. It is the state of healing the ills of the human being with natural, temperate living. It is maturation of the ego as it passes from a self-centered phase to its awareness and devotion to humanity.

It is humanitarian, pragmatic, and scientific, with boundless curiosity. Focus and clarity of mind are the strong points, while strength of purpose and shy reserve underlie the whole sign. There is separateness, aloofness, and solitude for this beacon of the Zodiac. As a lighthouse guides ships, so Virgo shines.

LIBRA
The Sign of the Scales

Libra is the sign of human relationship, marriage, equality, and justice. It symbolizes the need of one human being for another, the capacity to find light, warmth, and life-giving love in relationship to another human being. It is union on any level—mental, sexual, emotional, or business. It is self-extension in a desire to find a partner with whom to share our joys. It is the capacity to recognize the needs of others and to develop to the fullest our powers of diplomacy, good taste, and refinement.

Libra is harmony, grace, aesthetic sensibility, and the personification of the spirit of companionship. It represents the skill to maintain balances and the ability to share mutually all life's benefits, trials, crises, and blessings. Libra is mastery at anticipation of another's needs or reactions. It is the exercise of simple justice with impartial delicacy.

It is the need to relate, to find a major person, place, or thing to sustain us and draw out our attention. It is growth through becoming awakened to the outside world and other people. It is the union of two loving souls in honesty, equality, mutual cooperation, and mutual accord.

SCORPIO
The Sign of the Scorpion

Scorpio is the sign of dark intensity, swirling passion, and sexual magnetism. It is the thirst for survival and regeneration that are the bases of sexual orientation and the creative impulses for self-expression. No other sign has such a profound instinct for survival and reproduction. Out of the abyss of emotions come a thousand creations, each one possessing a life of its own.

Scorpio is completion, determination, and endurance, fortified with enough stamina to outlive any enemy. It is the pursuit of goals despite any threat, warning, or obstacle that might stand in the way. It simply cannot be stopped. It knows when to wait and when to proceed. It is the constant state of readiness, a vibrant living force that constantly pumps out its rhythm from the depths of being.

Secretive and intimate, Scorpio symbolizes the self-directed creature with a will of steel. It is the flaming desire to create, manipulate, and control with a magician's touch. But the most mysterious quality is the capacity for metamorphosis, or total transformation.

This represents supremacy in the battle with dark unseen forces. It is the state of being totally fearless—the embodiment of truth and courage. It symbolizes the human capacity to face all danger and emerge supreme, to heal oneself. As a caterpillar spins its way into the darkness of a cocoon, Scorpio faces the end of existence, says goodbye to an old way of life, and goes through a kind of death—or total change.

Then, amid the dread of uncertainty, something remarkable happens. From hopelessness or personal crisis a new individual emerges, like a magnificent butterfly leaving behind its cocoon. It is a human being completely transformed and victorious. This is Scorpio.

SAGITTARIUS
The Sign of the Archer

Sagittarius is the sign of adventure and a thousand and one new experiences. It is the cause and purpose of every new attempt at adventure or self-understanding. It is the embodiment of enthusiasm, search for truth, and love of wisdom. Hope and optimism characterize this section of the Zodiac, and it is the ability to leave the past behind and set out again with positive resilience and a happy, cheerful outlook.

It is intelligence and exuberance, youthful idealism, and the desire to expand all horizons. It is the constant hatching of dreams, the hunger for knowledge, travel and experience. The goal is exploration itself.

Sagittarius is generosity, humor, and goodness of nature, backed up by the momentum of great expectations. It symbolizes the ability of people to be back in the race after having the most serious spills over the biggest hurdles. It is a healthy, positive outlook and the capacity to meet each new moment with unaffected buoyancy.

At this point in the Zodiac, greater conscious understanding begins to develop self-awareness and self-acceptance. It is an Olympian capacity to look upon the bright side and to evolve that aspect of mind we call conscience.

CAPRICORN
The Sign of the Sea Goat

Capricorn is the sign of structure and physical law. It rules depth, focus, and concentration. It is the symbol of success through perseverance, happiness through profundity. It is victory over disruption, and finds reality in codes set up by society and culture. It is the perpetuation of useful, tested patterns and a desire to protect what has already been established.

It is cautious, conservative, conscious of the passage of time, yet ageless. The Goat symbolizes the incorporation of reason into living and depth into loving. Stability, responsibility, and fruitfulness through loyalty color this sector of the Zodiac with an undeniable and irrepressible awareness of success, reputation, and honor. Capricorn is the culmination of our earthly dreams, the pinnacle of our worldly life.

It is introspection and enlightenment through serious contemplation of the Self and its position in the world. It is mastery of understanding and the realization of dreams.

Capricorn is a winter blossom, a born professional with an aim of harmony and justice, beauty, grace, and success. It is the well-constructed pyramid: perfect and beautiful, architecturally correct, mysteriously implacable, and hard to know. It is highly organized and built on precise foundations to last and last and last. It is practical, useful yet magnificent and dignified, signifying permanence and careful planning. Like a pyramid, Capricorn has thick impenetrable walls, complex passageways, and false corridors. Yet somewhere at the heart of this ordered structure is the spirit of a mighty ruler.

AQUARIUS
The Sign of the Water Bearer

Aquarius is the symbol of idealized free society. It is the herding instinct in man as a social animal. It is the collection of heterogeneous elements of human consciousness in coherent peaceful coexistence. Friendship, goodwill, and harmonious contact are Aquarius attributes. It is founded on the principle of individual freedom and the brotherly love and respect for the rights of all men and women on Earth.

It is strength of will and purpose, altruism, and love of human fellowship. It is the belief in spontaneity and free choice, in the openness to live in a spirit of harmony and cooperation—liberated from restriction, repression, and conventional codes of conduct. It is the brilliant capacity to assimilate information instantaneously at the last minute and translate that information into immediate creative action, and so the result is to live in unpredictability.

This is the progressive mind, the collective mind—groups of people getting together to celebrate life. Aquarius is the child of the future, the utopian working for the betterment of the human race. Funds, charities, seeking better cities and better living conditions for others, involvement in great forms of media or communication, science or research in the hope of joining mankind to his higher self—this is all Aquarius.

It is invention, genius, revolution, discovery—instantaneous breakthrough from limitations. It's a departure from convention, eccentricity, the unexpected development that changes the course of history. It is the discovery of people and all the arteries that join them together. Aquarius is adventure, curiosity, exotic and alien appeal. It pours the water of life and intelligence for all humanity to drink. It is humanism, community, and the element of surprise.

PISCES
The Sign of the Fishes

Pisces is faith—undistracted, patient, all-forgiving faith—and therein lies the Pisces capacity for discipline, endurance, and stamina.

It is imagination and other-worldliness, the condition

of living a foggy, uncertain realm of poetry, music, and fantasy. Passive and compassionate, this sector of the Zodiac symbolizes the belief in the inevitability of life. It represents the view of life that everything exists in waves, like the sea. All reality as we know it is a dream, a magic illusion that must ultimately be washed away. Tides pull this way and that, whirlpools and undercurrents sweep across the bottom of life's existence, but in Pisces there is total acceptance of all tides, all rhythms, all possibilities. It is the final resolution of all personal contradictions and all confusing paradoxes.

It is the search for truth and honesty, and the devotion to love, utterly and unquestionably. It is the desire to act with wisdom, kindness, and responsibility and to welcome humanity completely free from scorn, malice, discrimination, or prejudice. It is total, all-embracing, idealistic love. It is the acceptance of two sides of a question at once and love through sacrifice.

Pisces is beyond reality. We are here today, but may be gone tomorrow. Let the tide of circumstances carry you where it will, for nothing is forever. As all things come, so must they go. In the final reel, all things must pass away. It is deliverance from sorrow through surrender to the infinite. The emotions are as vast as the ocean, yet in the pain of confusion there is hope in the secret cell of one's own heart. Pisces symbolizes liberation from pain through love, faith, and forgiveness.

THE SIGNS AND
THEIR KEY WORDS

		Positive	Negative
ARIES	self	courage, initiative, pioneer instinct	brash rudeness, selfish impetuosity
TAURUS	money	endurance, loyalty, wealth	obstinacy, gluttony
GEMINI	mind	versatility, communication	capriciousness, unreliability
CANCER	family	sympathy, homing instinct	clannishness, childishness
LEO	children	love, authority, integrity	egotism, force
VIRGO	work	purity, industry, analysis	faultfinding, cynicism
LIBRA	marriage	harmony, justice	vacillation, superficiality
SCORPIO	sex	survival, regeneration	vengeance, discord
SAGITTARIUS	travel	optimism, higher learning	lawlessness, irresponsibility
CAPRICORN	career	depth, responsibility	narrowness, gloom
AQUARIUS	friends	humanity, genius	perverse unpredictability
PISCES	faith	spiritual love, universality	diffusion, escapism

THE ELEMENTS AND
THE QUALITIES OF THE SIGNS

Every sign has both an element and a quality associated with it. The element indicates the basic makeup of the sign, and the quality describes the kind of activity associated with each.

Element	Sign	Quality	Sign
Fire	Aries Leo Sagittarius	Cardinal	Aries Libra Cancer Capricorn
Earth	Taurus Virgo Capricorn	Fixed	Taurus Leo Scorpio Aquarius
Air	Gemini Libra Aquarius	Mutable	Gemini Virgo Sagittarius Pisces
Water	Cancer Scorpio Pisces		

Signs can be grouped together according to their element and quality. Signs of the same element share many basic traits in common. They tend to form stable configurations and ultimately harmonious relationships. Signs of the same quality are often less harmonious, but share many dynamic potentials for growth and profound fulfillment.

The following pages describe these sign groupings in more detail.

The Fire Signs

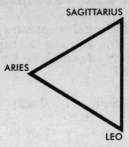

This is the fire group. On the whole these are emotional, volatile types, quick to anger, quick to forgive. They are adventurous, powerful people and act as a source of inspiration for everyone. They spark into action with immediate exuberant impulses. They are intelligent, self-involved, creative, and idealistic. They all share a certain vibrancy and glow that outwardly reflects an inner flame and passion for living.

The Earth Signs

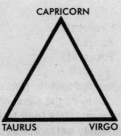

This is the earth group. They are in constant touch with the material world and tend to be conservative. Although they are all capable of spartan self-discipline, they are earthy, sensual people who are stimulated by the tangible, elegant, and luxurious. The thread of their lives is always practical, but they do fantasize and are often attracted to dark, mysterious, emotional people. They are like great cliffs overhanging the sea, forever married to the ocean but always resisting erosion from the dark, emotional forces that thunder at their feet.

The Air Signs

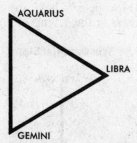

This is the air group. They are light, mental creatures desirous of contact, communication, and relationship. They are involved with people and the forming of ties on many levels. Original thinkers, they are the bearers of human news. Their language is their sense of word, color, style, and beauty. They provide an atmosphere suitable and pleasant for living. They add change and versatility to the scene, and it is through them that we can explore human intelligence and experience.

The Water Signs

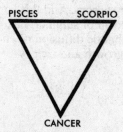

This is the water group. Through the water people, we are all joined together on emotional, nonverbal levels.

The water signs are silent, mysterious types whose magic hypnotizes even the most determined realist. They have uncanny perceptions about people and are as rich as the oceans when it comes to feeling, emotion, or imagination. They are sensitive, mystical creatures with memories that go back beyond time. Through water, life is sustained. These people have the potential for the depths of darkness or the heights of mysticism and art.

The Cardinal Signs

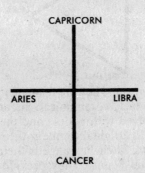

The cardinal signs present a picture of dynamism, activity, tremendous stress, and remarkable achievement. These people know the meaning of great change since their lives are often characterized by significant crises and major successes. The cardinal signs mark the beginning of the four seasons. And this combination is like a simultaneous storm of summer, fall, winter, and spring. The danger is chaotic diffusion of energy; the potential is irrepressible growth and victory.

The Fixed Signs

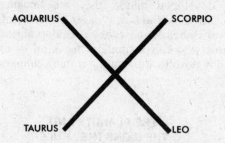

Fixed signs are always establishing themselves in a given place or area of experience. Like explorers who arrive and plant a flag, these people claim a position from which they do not enjoy being deposed. They are staunch, stalwart, upright, trusty, honorable people, although their obstinacy is well-known. Their contribution is fixity, and they are the angels who support our visible world.

The Mutable Signs

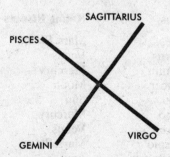

Mutable people are versatile, sensitive, intelligent, nervous, and deeply curious about life. They are the translators of all energy. They often carry out or complete tasks initiated by others. People from mutable signs have highly developed minds; they are imaginative and jumpy and think and talk a lot. At worst their lives are a Tower of Babel. At best they are adaptable and ready creatures who can assimilate one kind of experience and enjoy it while anticipating coming changes.

THE PLANETS AND
THE SIGNS THEY RULE

The signs of the Zodiac are linked to the planets in the following way. Each sign is governed or ruled by one or more planets. No matter where the planets are located in the sky at any given moment, they still rule their respective signs. When they travel through the signs they rule, they have special dignity and their effects are stronger.

Following is a list of the planets and the signs they rule. After you read the definitions of the planets from pages 88 to 96, see if you can determine how the planet ruling your Sun sign has affected your life.

Signs	Ruling Planets
Aries	Mars, Pluto
Taurus	Venus
Gemini	Mercury
Cancer	Moon
Leo	Sun
Virgo	Mercury
Libra	Venus
Scorpio	Mars, Pluto
Sagittarius	Jupiter
Capricorn	Saturn
Aquarius	Saturn, Uranus
Pisces	Jupiter, Neptune

THE ZODIAC AND
THE HUMAN BODY

The signs of the Zodiac are linked to the human body in a direct relationship. Each sign has a part of the body with which it is associated.

It is traditionally believed that surgery is best performed when the Moon is passing through a sign *other* than the sign associated with the part of the body upon which an operation is to be performed. But often the presence of the Moon in a particular sign will bring the focus of attention to that very part of the body under medical scrutiny.

The principles of medical astrology are complex and beyond the scope of this introduction. We can, however, list the signs of the Zodiac and the parts of the human body connected with them. Once you learn these correspondences, you'll be amazed at how accurate they are.

Signs	Human Body
Aries	Head, brain, face, upper jaw
Taurus	Throat, neck, lower jaw
Gemini	Hands, arms, lungs, nerves
Cancer	Stomach, breasts, womb, liver
Leo	Heart, spine
Virgo	Intestines, liver
Libra	Kidneys, lower back
Scorpio	Sex and eliminative organs
Sagittarius	Hips, thighs, liver
Capricorn	Skin, bones, teeth, knees
Aquarius	Circulatory system, lower legs
Pisces	Feet, tone of being

THE ZODIACAL HOUSES
AND THE RISING SIGN

Apart from the month and day of birth, the exact time of birth is another vital factor in the determination of an accurate horoscope. Not only do planets move with great speed, but one must know how far the Earth has turned during the day. That way you can determine exactly where the planets are located with respect to the precise birthplace of an individual. This makes your horoscope *your* horoscope.

The horoscope sets up a kind of framework around which the life of an individual grows like wild ivy, this way and that, weaving its way around the trellis of the natal positions of the planets. The year of birth tells us the positions of the distant, slow-moving planets Jupiter, Saturn, Uranus, Neptune, and Pluto. The month of birth indicates the Sun sign, or birth sign as it is commonly called, as well as indicating the positions of the rapidly moving planets Venus, Mercury, and Mars. The day of birth, as well as the time, locates the position of our Moon. And the moment of birth—the exact hour and minute—determines the houses through what is called the Ascendant, or Rising sign.

The illustration on the next page shows the flat chart, or natural wheel, an astrologer uses. The inner circle of the wheel is labeled 1 through 12. These 12 divisions are known as the houses of the Zodiac.

The 1st house always starts from the position marked E, which corresponds to the eastern horizon. The rest of the houses 2 through 12 follow around in a "counterclockwise" direction. The point where each house starts is known as a cusp, or edge.

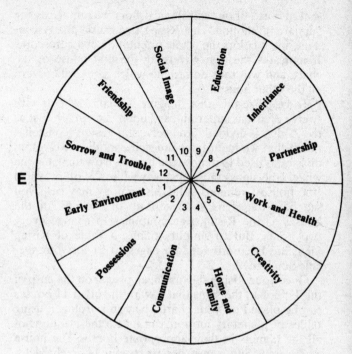

The 12 Houses of the Zodiac

The cusp, or edge, of the 1st house (point E) is where an astrologer would place your Rising sign, the Ascendant. The Rising sign is very important in a horoscope, as it defines your self-image, outlook, physical constitution, early environment, and whole orientation to life. And, as already mentioned, the exact time of your birth determines your Rising sign. Let's see how this works.

As the Earth rotates on its axis once every 24 hours, each one of the 12 signs of the Zodiac appears to be "rising" on the horizon, with a new one appearing about every two hours. Actually it is the turning of the Earth that exposes each sign to view, but you will remember that in much of our astrological work we are discussing "apparent" motion. This Rising sign marks the Ascendant, and it colors the whole orientation of a horoscope. It indicates the sign governing the first house of the chart, and will thus determine which signs will govern all the other houses.

To visualize this idea, imagine two color wheels with twelve divisions superimposed upon each other. Just as the Zodiac is divided into twelve star groups (constellations) that we identify as the signs, another twelvefold division is used to denote the houses. Now imagine one wheel (the signs) moving slowly while the other wheel (the houses) remains still. This analogy may help you see how the signs keep shifting the "color" of the houses as the Rising sign continues to change every two hours. But to simplify things, a Table of Rising Signs has been provided on pages 20–21 for your specific Sun sign.

Once your Rising sign has been placed on the cusp of the 1st house, the signs that govern the other 11 houses can be placed on your chart. Then an astrologer, using tables of planetary motion, can locate the positions of all the planets in their appropriate houses. The house where your Sun sign is describes your basic character and your fundamental drives. And the houses where the other planets are in your chart suggest the areas of life on Earth in which you will be most likely to focus your constant energy and center your activity.

The illustration on page 83 briefly identifies each of the 12 houses of the Zodiac. Now the pages that follow provide a detailed discussion of the meanings of the houses. In the section after the houses we will define all the known planets of the solar system, with a separate section on the Moon, in order to acquaint you with more of the astrological vocabulary you will be meeting again and again.

THE MEANING OF THE HOUSES

The twelve houses of every horoscope represent areas of life on Earth, or regions of worldly experience. Depending on which sign of the Zodiac was rising on the eastern horizon at the moment of birth, the activity of each house will be "colored" by the zodiacal sign on its cusp, or edge. In other words, the sign falling on the first house will determine what signs will fall on the rest of the houses.

1 The first house determines the basic orientation to all of life on Earth. It indicates the body type, face, head, and brain. It rules your self-image, or the way others see you because of the way you see your self. This is the Ascendant of the horoscope and is the focus of energies of your whole chart. It acts like a prism through which all of the planetary light passes and is reflected in your life. It colors your outlook and influences everything you do and see.

2 This is the house of finances. Here is your approach to money and materialism in general. It indicates where the best sources are for you to improve your financial condition and your earning power as a whole. It indicates chances for gain or loss. It describes your values, alliances, and assets.

3 This is the house of the day-to-day mind. Short trips, communication, and transportation are associated with this house. It deals with routines, brothers and sisters, relatives, neighbors, and the near environment at hand. Language, letters, and the tools for transmitting information are included in third-house matters.

4 This is the house that describes your home and home life, parents, and childhood in the sense of indicating the kind of roots you come from. It symbolizes your present home and domestic situation and reflects your need for privacy and retreat from the world, indicating, of course, what kind of scene you require.

5   Pleasure, love affairs, amusements, parties, creativity, children. This is the house of passion and courtship and of expressing your talents, whatever they are. It is related to the development of your personal life and the capacity to express feeling and enjoy romance.

6   This is the house of work. Here there are tasks to be accomplished and maladjustments to be corrected. It is the house of health as well, and describes some of the likely places where physical health difficulties may appear. It rules routines, regimen, necessary jobs as opposed to a chosen career, army, navy, police—people employed, co-workers, and those in service to others. It indicates the individual's ability to harvest the fruit of his own efforts.

7   This is the house of marriage, partnership, and unions. It represents the alter ego, all people other than yourself, open confrontation with the public. It describes your partner and the condition of partnership as you discern it. In short, it is your "take" on the world. It indicates your capacity to make the transition from courtship to marriage and specifically what you seek out in others.

8   This is the house of deep personal transition, sex as a form of mutual surrender and interchange between human beings. It is the release from tensions and the completion of the creative processes. The eighth house also has to do with taxes, inheritances, and the finances of others, as well as death as the ending of cycles and crises.

9   This is the house of the higher mind, philosophy, religion, and the expression of personal conscience through moral codes. It indicates political leanings, ethical views, and the capacity of the individual for a broader perspective and deeper understanding of himself in relation to society. It is through the ninth house that you make great strides in learning and travel to distant places and come to know yourself through study, dreams, and wide experience.

10 This is the house of career, honor, and prestige. It marks the culmination of worldly experience and indicates the highest point you can reach, what you look up to, and how high you can go in this lifetime. It describes your parents, employers, and how you view authority figures, the condition and direction of your profession, and your position in the community.

11 This is the house of friendships. It describes your social behavior, your views on humanity, and your hopes, aspirations, and wishes for an ideal life. It will indicate what kinds of groups, clubs, organizations, and friendships you tend to form and what you seek out in your chosen alliances other than with your mate or siblings. This house suggests the capacity for the freedom and unconventionality that an individual is seeking, his sense of his connection with mankind, and the definition of his goals, personal and social.

12 This is the house of seclusion, secret wisdom, and self-incarceration. It indicates our secret enemies as well, in the sense that there may be persons, feelings, or memories we are trying to escape. It is self-undoing in that this house acts against the ego in order to find a higher, more universal purpose. It rules prisons, hospitals, charities, and selfless service. It is the house of unfinished psychic business.

THE PLANETS OF THE SOLAR SYSTEM

The planets of the solar system all travel around the Sun at different speeds and different distances. Taken with the Sun, they all distribute individual intelligence and ability throughout the entire chart.

The planets modify the influence of the Sun in a chart according to their own particular natures, strengths, and positions. Their positions must be calculated for each year and day, and their function and expression in a horoscope will change as they move from one area of the Zodiac to another.

Following, you will find brief statements of their pure meanings.

THE SUN

The Sun is the center of existence. Around this flaming sphere all the planets revolve in endless orbits. Our star is constantly sending out its beams of light and energy without which no life on Earth would be possible. In astrology it symbolizes everything we are trying to become, the center around which all of our activity in life will always revolve. It is the symbol of our basic nature and describes the natural and constant thread that runs through everything that we do from birth to death on this planet.

Everything in the horoscope ultimately revolves around this singular body. Although other forces may be prominent in the charts of some individuals, still the Sun is the total nucleus of being and symbolizes the

THE SUN

complete potential of every human being alive. It is vitality and the life force. Your whole essence comes from the position of the Sun.

You are always trying to express the Sun according to its position by house and sign. Possibility for all development is found in the Sun, and it marks the fundamental character of your personal radiations all around you.

It symbolizes strength, vigor, ardor, generosity, and the ability to function effectively as a mature individual and a creative force in society. It is consciousness of the gift of life. The undeveloped solar nature is arrogant pushy, undependable, and proud, and is constantly using force.

MERCURY

Mercury is the planet closest to the Sun. It races around our star, gathering information and translating it to the rest of the system. Mercury represents your capacity to understand the desires of your own will and to translate those desires into action.

MERCURY

In other words it is the planet of mind and the power of communication. Through Mercury we develop an ability to think, write, speak, and observe—to become aware of the world around us. It colors our attitudes and vision of the world, as well as our capacity to communicate our inner responses to the outside world. Some people who have serious disabilities in their power of verbal communication have often wrongly been described as people lacking intelligence.

Although this planet (and its position in the horoscope) indicates your power to communicate your thoughts and perceptions to the world, intelligence is something deeper. Intelligence is distributed throughout all the planets. It is the relationship of the planets to each other that truly describes what we call intelligence. Mercury rules speaking, language, mathematics, draft and design, students, messengers, young people, offices, teachers, and any pursuits where the mind of man has wings.

VENUS

Venus is beauty. It symbolizes the harmony and radiance of a rare and elusive quality: beauty itself. It is refinement and delicacy, softness and charm. In astrology it indicates grace, balance, and the aesthetic sense. Where Venus is we see beauty, a gentle drawing in of energy and the need for satisfaction and completion. It is a special touch that finishes off rough edges.

VENUS

Venus is the planet of sensitivity and affection, and it is always the place for that other elusive phenomenon:

love. Venus describes our sense of what is beautiful and loving. Poorly developed, it is vulgar, tasteless, and self-indulgent. But its ideal is the flame of spiritual love—Aphrodite, goddess of love, and the sweetness and power of personal beauty.

MARS

Mars is raw, crude energy. The planet next to Earth but outward from the Sun is a fiery red sphere that charges through the horoscope with force and fury. It represents the way you reach out for new adventure and new experience. It is energy drive, initiative, courage, daring. It is the power to start something and see it through. It can be thoughtless, cruel and wild, angry and hostile, causing cuts, burns, scalds, wounds. It can stab its way through a chart, or it can be the symbol of healthy spirited adventure, well-channeled constructive power to begin and keep up the drive.

MARS

If you have trouble starting things, if you lack the get-up-and-go to start the ball rolling, if you lack aggressiveness and self-confidence, chances are there's another planet influencing your Mars. Mars rules soldiers, butchers, surgeons, salespeople—in general any field that requires daring, bold skill, operational technique, or self-promotion.

JUPITER

Jupiter is the largest planet of the solar system. Planet Jupiter rules good luck and good cheer, health, wealth, optimism, happiness, success, joy. It is the symbol of opportunity and always opens the way for new possibilities in your life. It rules exuberance, enthusiasm, wisdom, knowledge, generosity, and all forms of expansion in general. It rules actors, statesmen, clerics, professional people, religion, publishing, and the distribution of many people over large areas.

JUPITER

Sometimes Jupiter makes you think you deserve everything, and you become sloppy, wasteful, careless and rude, prodigal and lawless, in the illusion that nothing can ever go wrong. Then there is the danger of your showing overconfidence, exaggeration, undependability, and overindulgence.

Jupiter is the minimization of limitation and the emphasis on spirituality and potential. It is the thirst for knowledge and higher learning.

SATURN

Saturn circles our system in dark splendor with its mysterious rings, forcing us to be awakened to whatever we have neglected in the past. It will present real puzzles and problems to be solved, causing delays, obstacles, and hindrances. By doing so, Saturn stirs our own sensitivity to those areas where we are laziest.

SATURN

Here we must patiently develop method, and only through painstaking effort can our ends be achieved. It brings order to a horoscope and imposes reason just where we are feeling least reasonable. By creating limitations and boundary, Saturn shows the consequences of being human and demands that we accept the changing cycles inevitable in human life. Saturn rules time, old age, and sobriety. It can bring depression, gloom, jealousy, and greed, or serious acceptance of responsibilities out of which success will develop. With Saturn there is nothing to do but face facts. It rules laborers, stones, granite, rocks, and crystals.

THE OUTER PLANETS: URANUS, NEPTUNE, PLUTO

Uranus, Neptune, and Pluto are the outer planets. They liberate human beings from cultural conditioning, and in that sense are the lawbreakers. In early times it was thought that Saturn was the last planet of the solar system—the outer limit beyond which we could never go. The discovery of the next three planets beyond Saturn ushered in new phases of human history, revolution, and technology.

URANUS

Uranus rules unexpected change, upheaval, revolution. It is the symbol of total independence and asserts the freedom of an individual from all restriction and restraint. It is a breakthrough planet and indicates talent, originality, and genius in a horoscope. It usually causes last-minute reversals and changes of plan, unwanted separations, accidents, catastrophes, and eccentric behavior. It can add irrational rebelliousness and perverse bohemianism to a personality or a streak of unaffected brilliance in science and art.

URANUS

Uranus rules technology, aviation, and all forms of electrical and electronic advancement. It governs great leaps forward and topsy-turvy situations, and always turns things around at the last minute. Its effects are difficult to predict, since it rules sudden last-minute decisions and events that come like lightning out of the blue.

NEPTUNE

Neptune dissolves existing reality the way the sea erodes the cliffs beside it. Its effects are subtle like the ringing of a buoy's bell in the fog. It suggests a reality higher than definition can usually describe. It awakens a sense of higher responsibility often causing guilt, worry, anxieties, or delusions. Neptune is associated with all forms of escape and can make things seem a certain way so convincingly that you are absolutely sure of something that eventually turns out to be quite different.

NEPTUNE

It is the planet of illusion and therefore governs the invisible realms that lie beyond our ordinary minds, beyond our simple factual ability to prove what is "real." Treachery, deceit, disillusionment, and disappointment are linked to Neptune. It describes a vague reality that promises eternity and the divine, yet in a manner so complex that we cannot really fathom it at all. At its worst Neptune is a cheap intoxicant; at its best it is the poetry, music, and inspiration of the higher planes of spiritual love. It has dominion over movies, photographs, and much of the arts.

PLUTO

Pluto lies at the outpost of our system and therefore rules finality in a horoscope—the final closing of chapters in your life, the passing of major milestones and points of development from which there is no return. It is a final wipeout, a closeout, an evacuation. It is a subtle but powerful catalyst in all transformations that occur. It creates, destroys, then recreates. Sometimes Pluto starts its influence with a minor event or insignificant incident that might even go unnoticed. Slowly but surely, little by little, everything changes, until at last there has been a total transformation in the area of your life where Pluto has been operating. It rules mass thinking and the trends that society first rejects, then adopts, and finally outgrows.

PLUTO

Pluto rules the dead and the underworld—all the powerful forces of creation and destruction that go on all the time beneath, around, and above us. It can bring a lust for power with strong obsessions.

It is the planet that rules the metamorphosis of the caterpillar into a butterfly, for it symbolizes the capacity to change totally and forever a person's lifestyle, way of thought, and behavior.

THE MOON

Exactly how does the Moon affect us psychologically and psychically? We know it controls the tides. We understand how it affects blood rhythm and body tides, together with all the chemical fluids that constitute our physical selves. Astronauts have walked upon its surface, and our scientists are now studying and analyzing data that will help determine the age of our satellite, its origin, and makeup.

THE MOON

But the true mystery of that small body as it circles our Earth each month remains hidden. Is it really a dead, lifeless body that has no light or heat of its own, reflecting only what the gigantic Sun throws toward it? Is it a sensitive reflecting device, which translates the blinding, billowing energy from our star into a language our bodies can understand?

In astrology, the Moon is said to rule our feelings, customs, habits, and moods. As the Sun is the constant, ever shining source of life in daytime, the Moon is our nighttime mother, lighting up the night and swiftly moving, reflecting ever so rapidly the changing phases of behavior and personality. If we feel happy or joyous, or we notice certain habits and repetitive feelings that bubble up from our dark centers then vanish as quickly as they appeared, very often it is the position of the Moon that describes these changes.

THE MOON IN ALL SIGNS

The Moon moves quickly through the Zodiac, that is, through all twelve signs of our Sun's apparent path. It stays in each sign for about 2¼ days. During its brief stay in a given sign, the moods and responses of people are always colored by the nature of that sign, any planets located there at that time, or any other heavenly bodies placed in such a way that the Moon will pick up their "vibration" as well. It's astonishing to observe how clearly the Moon changes people's interests and involvements as it moves along.

The following section gives brief descriptions of the Moon's influence in each sign.

MOON IN ARIES

There's excitement in the air. Some new little thing appears, and people are quick and full of energy and enterprise, ready for something new and turning on to a new experience. There's not much patience or hesitation, doubt or preoccupation with guilty self-damning recriminations. What's needed is action. People feel like putting their plans into operation. Pleasure and adventure characterize the mood, and it's time for things to change, pick up, improve. Confidence, optimism, positive feeling pervade the air. Sick people take a turn for the better. Life stirs with a feeling of renewal. People react bravely to challenges, with a sense of courage and dynamism. Self-reliance is the key word, and people minimize their problems and maximize the power to exercise freedom of the will. There is an air of abruptness and shortness of consideration, as people are feeling the courage of their convictions to do something for themselves. Feelings are strong and intuitive, and the mood is idealistic and freedom-oriented.

MOON IN TAURUS

Here the mood is just as pleasure loving, but less idealistic. Now the concerns are more materialistic, money-oriented, down-to-earth. The mood is stable, diligent, thoughtful, deliberate. It is a time when feelings are rich and deep, with a profound appreciation of the good things the world has to offer and the pleasures of the sensations. It is a period when people's minds are serious, realistic, and devoted to the increases and improvements of property and possessions and acquisition of wealth. There is a conservative tone, and people are fixed in their views, needing to add to their stability in every way. Assessment of assets, criticism, and the execution of tasks are strong involvements of the Taurus Moon when financial matters demand attention. It is devotion to security on a financial and emotional level. It is a fertile time, when ideas can begin to take root and grow.

MOON IN GEMINI

There is a rapid increase in movement. People are going places, exchanging ideas and information. Gossip and news travel fast under a Gemini Moon, because people are naturally involved with communication, finding out things from some, passing on information to others. Feelings shift to a mental level now, and people feel and say things that are sincere at the moment but lack the root and depth to endure much beyond the moment. People are involved with short-term engagements, quick trips. There is a definite need for changing the scene. You'll find people flirtatious and talkative, experimental and easygoing, falling into encounters they hadn't planned on. The mind is quick and active, with powers of writing and speaking greatly enhanced. Radio, television, letters, newspapers, magazines are in the spotlight with the Moon in Gemini, and new chances pop up for self-expression, with new people involved. Relatives and neighbors are tuned in to you and you to them. Take advantage of this fluidity of mind. It can rescue you from worldly involvements and get you into new surroundings for a short while.

MOON IN CANCER

Now you'll see people heading home. People turn their attention inward to their place of residence under a Cancer Moon. The active, changeable moods of yesterday vanish, and people settle in as if they were searching for a nest of security. Actually people are retiring, seeking to find peace and quiet within themselves. That's what they're feeling when they prefer to stay home rather than go out with a crowd of people to strange places. They need the warmth and comfort of the family and hearth. Maybe they feel anxious and insecure from the hustle and bustle of the workaday world. Maybe they're just tired. But it's definitely a time of tender need for emotional sustenance. It's a time for nostalgia and returning to times and places that once nourished deeply. Thoughts of parents, family, and old associations come to people. The heritage of their family ties holds them strongly now. These are personal needs that must be fed. Moods are deep and mysterious and sometimes sad. People are silent, psychic, and imaginative during this period. It's a fruitful time when people respond to love, food, and all the comforts of the inner world.

MOON IN LEO

The shift is back out in the world, and people are born again, like kids. They feel zestful, passionate, exuberant and need plenty of attention. They're interested in having a good time, enjoying themselves, and the world of entertainment takes over for a while. Places of amusement, theaters, parties, sprees, a whole gala of glamorous events, characterize this stage of the Moon's travel. Gracious, lavish hosting and a general feeling of buoyancy and flamboyance are in the air. It's a time of sunny, youthful fun when people are in the mood to take chances and win. The approach is direct, ardent, and strong. Bossy, authoritarian feelings predominate, and people throw themselves forward for all they're worth. Flattery is rampant, but the ego is vibrant and flourishing with the kiss of life, romance, and love. Speculation is indicated, and it's usually a time to go out and try your hand at love. Life is full and rich as a summer meadow, and feelings are warm.

MOON IN VIRGO

The party's over. Eyelashes are on the table. This is a time for cleaning up after the merrymakers have gone home. People are now concerned with sobering up and getting personal affairs straight, clearing up any confusions or undefined feelings from the night before, and generally attending to the practical business of doctoring up after the party. People are back at work, concerned with necessary, perhaps tedious tasks—paying bills, fixing and adjusting things, and generally purifying their lives, streamlining their affairs, and involving themselves with work and service to the community. Purity is the key word in personal habits, diet, and emotional needs. Propriety and coolness take the place of yesterday's devil-may-care passion, and the results are a detached, inhibited period under a Virgo Moon.

Feelings are not omitted; they are merely subjected to the scrutiny of the mind and thus purified. Health comes to the fore, and people are interested in clearing up problems.

MOON IN LIBRA

Here there is a mood of harmony, when people strive to join with other people in a bond of peace and justice. At this time people need relationships and often seek the company of others in a smooth-flowing feeling of love, beauty, and togetherness. People make efforts to understand other people, and though it's not the best time to make decisions, many situations keep presenting themselves from the outside to change plans and offer new opportunities. There is a general search for accord between partners, and differences are explored as similarities are shared. The tone is concilatory, and the mood is one of cooperation, patience, and tolerance. People do not generally feel independent, and sometimes this need to share or lean on others disturbs them. It shouldn't. This is the moment for uniting and sharing, for feeling a mutual flow of kindness and tenderness between people. The air is ingratiating and sometimes lacks stamina, courage, and a consistent, definite point of view. But it is a time favoring the condition of beauty and the development of all forms of art.

MOON IN SCORPIO

This is not a mood of sharing. It's driving, intense, brooding—full of passion and desire. Its baser aspects are the impulses of selfishness, cruelty, and the pursuit of animal drives and appetites. There is a craving for excitement and a desire to battle and win in a bloodthirsty war for survival. It is competitive and ruthless, sarcastic and easily bruised, highly sexual and touchy, without being especially tender. Retaliation, jealousy, and revenge can be felt too during this time. Financial involvements, debts, and property issues arise now. Powerful underworld forces are at work here, and great care is needed to transform ignorance into wisdom, to keep the mind from descending into the lower depths. During the Moon's stay in Scorpio we contact the dark undercurrents swirling around and get in touch with a magical part of our natures. Interest lies in death, inheritance, and the powers of rebirth and regeneration.

MOON IN SAGITTARIUS

Here the mind climbs out of the depths, and people are involved with the higher, more enlightened, and conscious facets of their personality. There's a renewed interest in learning, education, and philosophy, and a new involvement with ethics, morals, national and international issues: a concern with looking for a better way to live. It's a time of general improvement, with people feeling more deeply hopeful and optimistic. They are dreaming of new places, new possibilities, new horizons. They are emerging from the abyss and leaving the past behind, with their eyes gazing toward the new horizon. They decide to travel, or renew their contacts with those far away. They question their religious beliefs and investigate new areas of metaphysical inquiry. It's a time for adventure, sports, playing the field—people have their eye on new possibilities. They are bored with depression and details. They feel restless and optimistic, joyous and delighted to be alive. Thoughts revolve around adventure, travel, liberation.

MOON IN CAPRICORN

When the Moon moves into Capricorn, things slow down considerably. People require a quiet, organized, and regularized condition. Their minds are sober and realistic, and they are methodically going about bringing their dreams and plans into reality. They are more conscious of what is standing between them and success, and during this time they take definite, decisive steps to remove any obstacles from their path. They are cautious, suspicious, sometimes depressed, discouraged, and gloomy, but they are more determined than ever to accomplish their tasks. They take care of responsibilities now, wake up to facts, and wrestle with problems and dilemmas of this world. They are politically minded and concerned with social convention now, and it is under a Capricorn Moon that conditioning and conformity elicit the greatest responses. People are moderate and serious and surround themselves with what is most familiar. They want predictable situations and need time to think deeply and deliberately about all issues. It's a time for planning.

MOON IN AQUARIUS

Spontaneity replaces the sober predictability of yesterday. Now events, people, and situations pop up, and you take advantage of unsought opportunities and can expect the unexpected. Surprises, reversals, and shifts in plans mark this period. There is a resurgence of optimism, and things you wouldn't expect to happen suddenly do. What you were absolutely sure was going to happen simply doesn't. Here there is a need for adventure born from a healthy curiosity that characterizes people's moods. Unrealistic utopias are dreamed of, and it is from such idealistic dreams that worlds of the future are built. There is a renewed interest in friendship, comradeship, community, and union on high planes of mental and spiritual companionship. People free each other from grudges or long-standing dead-locks, and there is a hopeful joining of hands in a spirit of love and peace. People don't feel like sticking to previous plans, and they must be able to respond to new situations at the last minute. People need freedom. Groups of people come together and meet, perhaps for a common purpose of having dinner or hearing music, and leave knowing each other better.

MOON IN PISCES

Flashes of brilliant insight and mysterious knowledge characterize the Moon's passage in Pisces. Sometimes valuable "truths" seem to emerge which, later in the light of day, turn out to be false. This is a time of poetry, intuition, and music, when worldly realities can be the most illusory and unreliable of all. There are often feelings of remorse, guilt, or sorrow connected with a Pisces Moon—sorrow from the childhood or family or past. Confusion, anxiety, worry, and a host of imagined pains and sorrows may drag you down until you cannot move or think. Often there are connections with hospitals, prisons, alcohol, drugs, and lower forms of escape. It is a highly emotional time, when the feelings and compassion for humanity and all people everywhere rise to the surface of your being. Mysteries of society and the soul now rise to demand solutions, but often the riddles posed during this period have many answers that all seem right. It is more a time for inner reflection than positive action. It is a time when poetry and music float to the surface of the being, and for the creative artist it is the richest source of inspiration.

MOON TABLES

CORRECTION FOR NEW YORK TIME, FIVE HOURS WEST OF GREENWICH

Atlanta, Boston, Detroit, Miami, Washington, Montreal,
Ottawa, Quebec, Bogota,
Havana, Lima, Santiago . . . . Same time

Chicago, New Orleans, Houston, Winnipeg, Churchill,
Mexico City . . . . Deduct 1 hour

Albuquerque, Denver, Phoenix, El Paso, Edmonton,
Helena . . . . Deduct 2 hours

Los Angeles, San Francisco, Reno, Portland,
Seattle, Vancouver . . . . Deduct 3 hours

Honolulu, Anchorage, Fairbanks, Kodiak . . . . Deduct 5 hours

Nome, Samoa, Tonga, Midway . . . . Deduct 6 hours

Halifax, Bermuda, San Juan, Caracas, La Paz,
Barbados . . . . Add 1 hour

St. John's, Brasilia, Rio de Janeiro, Sao Paulo,
Buenos Aires, Montevideo . . . . Add 2 hours

Azores, Cape Verde Islands . . . . Add 3 hours

Canary Islands, Madeira, Reykjavik . . . . Add 4 hours

London, Paris, Amsterdam, Madrid, Lisbon,
Gibraltar, Belfast, Rabat . . . . Add 5 hours

Frankfurt, Rome, Oslo, Stockholm, Prague,
Belgrade . . . . Add 6 hours

Bucharest, Beirut, Tel Aviv, Athens, Istanbul, Cairo,
Alexandria, Cape Town, Johannesburg . . . . Add 7 hours

Moscow, Leningrad, Baghdad, Dhahran,
Addis Ababa, Nairobi, Teheran, Zanzibar . . . . Add 8 hours

Bombay, Calcutta, Sri Lanka . . . . Add 10½ hours

Hong Kong, Shanghai, Manila, Peking,
Perth . . . . Add 13 hours

Tokyo, Okinawa, Darwin, Pusan . . . . Add 14 hours

Sydney, Melbourne, Port Moresby, Guam . . . . . . Add 15 hours

Auckland, Wellington, Suva, Wake . . . . Add 17 hours

2007 MOON SIGN DATES—NEW YORK TIME

JANUARY			FEBRUARY			MARCH		
Day	**Moon Enters**		**Day**	**Moon Enters**		**Day**	**Moon Enters**	
1.	Gemini		1.	Leo	12:16 am	1.	Leo	
2.	Cancer	10:15 am	2.	Leo		2.	Virgo	4:33 pm
3.	Cancer		3.	Virgo	9:35 am	3.	Virgo	
4.	Leo	5:15 pm	4.	Virgo		4.	Virgo	
5.	Leo		5.	Libra	9:16 pm	5.	Libra	4:26 am
6.	Leo		6.	Libra		6.	Libra	
7.	Virgo	1:19 am	7.	Libra		7.	Scorp.	5:18 pm
8.	Virgo		8.	Scorp.	10:11 am	8.	Scorp.	
9.	Libra	1:16 pm	9.	Scorp.		9.	Scorp.	
10.	Libra		10.	Sagitt.	10:02 pm	10.	Sagitt.	5:36 am
11.	Libra		11.	Sagitt.		11.	Sagitt.	
12.	Scorp.	2:09 am	12.	Sagitt.		12.	Capric.	3:36 pm
13.	Scorp.		13.	Capric.	6:43 am	13.	Capric.	
14.	Sagitt.	1:12 pm	14.	Capric.		14.	Aquar.	9:53 pm
15.	Sagitt.		15.	Aquar.	11:36 am	15.	Aquar.	
16.	Capric.	8:50 pm	16.	Aquar.		16.	Aquar.	
17.	Capric.		17.	Pisces	1:31 pm	17.	Pisces	12:31 am
18.	Capric.		18.	Pisces		18.	Pisces	
19.	Aquar.	1:17 am	19.	Aries	2:07 pm	19.	Aries	12:43 am
20.	Aquar.		20.	Aries		20.	Aries	
21.	Pisces	3:49 am	21.	Taurus	3:04 pm	21.	Taurus	12:16 am
22.	Pisces		22.	Taurus		22.	Taurus	
23.	Aries	5:53 am	23.	Gemini	5:43 pm	23.	Gemini	1:07 am
24.	Aries		24.	Gemini		24.	Gemini	
25.	Taurus	8:30 am	25.	Cancer	10:49 pm	25.	Cancer	4:50 am
26.	Taurus		26.	Cancer		26.	Cancer	
27.	Gemini	12:11 pm	27.	Cancer		27.	Leo	12:05 pm
28.	Gemini		28.	Leo	6:31 am	28.	Leo	
29.	Cancer	5:17 pm				29.	Virgo	10:28 pm
30.	Cancer					30.	Virgo	
31.	Cancer					31.	Virgo	

Daylight saving time to be considered where applicable.

2007 MOON SIGN DATES—NEW YORK TIME

APRIL
Day Moon Enters
1. Libra 10:44 am
2. Libra
3. Scorp. 11:37 pm
4. Scorp.
5. Scorp.
6. Sagitt. 11:58 am
7. Sagitt.
8. Capric. 10:37 pm
9. Capric.
10. Capric.
11. Aquar. 6:24 am
12. Aquar.
13. Pisces 10:40 am
14. Pisces
15. Aries 11:48 am
16. Aries
17. Taurus 11:12 am
18. Taurus
19. Gemini 10:52 am
20. Gemini
21. Cancer 12:51 pm
22. Cancer
23. Leo 6:39 pm
24. Leo
25. Leo
26. Virgo 4:25 am
27. Virgo
28. Libra 4:46 pm
29. Libra
30. Libra

MAY
Day Moon Enters
1. Scorp. 5:42 am
2. Scorp.
3. Sagitt. 5:49 pm
4. Sagitt.
5. Sagitt.
6. Capric. 4:22 am
7. Capric.
8. Aquar. 12:49 pm
9. Aquar.
10. Pisces 6:33 pm
11. Pisces
12. Aries 9:20 pm
13. Aries
14. Taurus 9:49 pm
15. Taurus
16. Gemini 9:35 pm
17. Gemini
18. Cancer 10:39 pm
19. Cancer
20. Cancer
21. Leo 2:58 am
22. Leo
23. Virgo 11:27 am
24. Virgo
25. Libra 11:17 pm
26. Libra
27. Libra
28. Scorp. 12:12 pm
29. Scorp.
30. Scorp.
31. Sagitt. 12:06 am

JUNE
Day Moon Enters
1. Sagitt.
2. Capric. 10:10 am
3. Capric.
4. Aquar. 6:16 pm
5. Aquar.
6. Aquar.
7. Pisces 12:25 am
8. Pisces
9. Aries 4:27 am
10. Aries
11. Taurus 6:30 am
12. Taurus
13. Gemini 7:25 am
14. Gemini
15. Cancer 8:46 am
16. Cancer
17. Leo 12:26 pm
18. Leo
19. Virgo 7:47 pm
20. Virgo
21. Virgo
22. Libra 5:45 am
23. Libra
24. Scorp. 7:26 pm
25. Scorp.
26. Scorp.
27. Sagitt. 7:25 pm
28. Sagitt.
29. Capric. 5:06 pm
30. Capric.

Daylight saving time to be considered where applicable.

2007 MOON SIGN DATES—NEW YORK TIME

JULY Day Moon Enters		AUGUST Day Moon Enters		SEPTEMBER Day Moon Enters	
1. Capric.		1. Pisces		1. Taurus	12:36 am
2. Aquar.	12:25 am	2. Aries	3:44 pm	2. Taurus	
3. Aquar.		3. Aries		3. Gemini	2:31 am
4. Pisces	5:53 am	4. Taurus	6:17 pm	4. Gemini	
5. Pisces		5. Taurus		5. Cancer	6:09 am
6. Aries	9:58 am	6. Gemini	9:02 pm	6. Cancer	
7. Aries		7. Gemini		7. Leo	12:00 pm
8. Taurus	12:55 pm	8. Gemini		8. Leo	
9. Taurus		9. Cancer	12:37 am	9. Virgo	8:11 pm
10. Gemini	3:11 pm	10. Cancer		10. Virgo	
11. Gemini		11. Leo	5:43 am	11. Virgo	
12. Cancer	5:40 pm	12. Leo		12. Libra	6:32 am
13. Cancer		13. Virgo	1:04 pm	13. Libra	
14. Leo	9:44 pm	14. Virgo		14. Scorp.	6:38 pm
15. Leo		15. Libra	11:05 pm	15. Scorp.	
16. Leo		16. Libra		16. Scorp.	
17. Virgo	4:40 am	17. Libra		17. Sagitt.	7:22 am
18. Virgo		18. Scorp.	11:14 am	18. Sagitt.	
19. Libra	2:54 pm	19. Scorp.		19. Capric.	6:53 pm
20. Libra		20. Sagitt.	11:45 pm	20. Capric.	
21. Libra		21. Sagitt.		21. Capric.	
22. Scorp.	3:19 am	22. Sagitt.		22. Aquar.	3:19 am
23. Scorp.		23. Capric.	10:21 am	23. Aquar.	
24. Sagitt.	3:31 pm	24. Capric.		24. Pisces	7:56 am
25. Sagitt.		25. Aquar.	5:36 pm	25. Pisces	
26. Sagitt.		26. Aquar.		26. Aries	9:24 am
27. Capric.	1:22 am	27. Pisces	9:35 pm	27. Aries	
28. Capric.		28. Pisces		28. Taurus	9:18 am
29. Aquar.	8:15 am	29. Aries	11:26 pm	29. Taurus	
30. Aquar.		30. Aries		30. Gemini	9:35 am
31. Pisces	12:42 pm	31. Aries			

Daylight saving time to be considered where applicable.

2007 MOON SIGN DATES—NEW YORK TIME

OCTOBER Day Moon Enters		NOVEMBER Day Moon Enters		DECEMBER Day Moon Enters	
1. Gemini		1. Leo		1. Virgo	
2. Cancer	11:58 am	2. Leo		2. Virgo	
3. Cancer		3. Virgo	7:46 am	3. Libra	1:02 am
4. Leo	5:26 pm	4. Virgo		4. Libra	
5. Leo		5. Libra	6:48 pm	5. Scorp.	1:32 pm
6. Leo		6. Libra		6. Scorp.	
7. Virgo	2:04 am	7. Libra		7. Scorp.	
8. Virgo		8. Scorp.	7:19 am	8. Sagitt.	2:12 am
9. Libra	12:59 pm	9. Scorp.		9. Sagitt.	
10. Libra		10. Sagitt.	8:00 pm	10. Capric.	1:52 pm
11. Libra		11. Sagitt.		11. Capric.	
12. Scorp.	1:14 am	12. Sagitt.		12. Capric.	
13. Scorp.		13. Capric.	8:02 am	13. Aquar.	12:02 am
14. Sagitt.	1:59 pm	14. Capric.		14. Aquar.	
15. Sagitt.		15. Aquar.	6:31 pm	15. Pisces	8:16 am
16. Sagitt.		16. Aquar.		16. Pisces	
17. Capric.	2:04 am	17. Aquar.		17. Aries	1:54 pm
18. Capric.		18. Pisces	2:16 am	18. Aries	
19. Aquar.	11:52 am	19. Pisces		19. Taurus	4:39 pm
20. Aquar.		20. Aries	6:25 am	20. Taurus	
21. Pisces	6:03 pm	21. Aries		21. Gemini	5:15 pm
22. Pisces		22. Taurus	7:20 am	22. Gemini	
23. Aries	8:25 pm	23. Taurus		23. Cancer	5:19 pm
24. Aries		24. Gemini	6:30 am	24. Cancer	
25. Taurus	8:06 pm	25. Gemini		25. Leo	6:53 pm
26. Taurus		26. Cancer	6:08 am	26. Leo	
27. Gemini	7:12 pm	27. Cancer		27. Virgo	11:45 pm
28. Gemini		28. Leo	8:24 am	28. Virgo	
29. Cancer	7:51 pm	29. Leo		29. Virgo	
30. Cancer		30. Virgo	2:45 pm	30. Libra	8:38 am
31. Leo	11:49 pm			31. Libra	

Daylight saving time to be considered where applicable.

2007 FISHING GUIDE

	Good	Best
January	1-5-6-19-25	2-3-4-11-30-31
February	1-2-3-4-17-24-28	16-26-27
March	1-2-3-4-11-18-30-31	5-6-25-26
April	17-24-29	2-3-4-5-9-29-30
May	4-5-10-24-31	1-2-15-29-30
June	1-2-14-28-29	3-4-8-23-26-30
July	2-3-7-27-29-30-31	13-23-28
August	2-12-20-26-27-30-31	1-5-24-28-29
September	4-11-22-23-26-27-28	20-24-25-29
October	18-24-25-28-29	3-10-22-26-27
November	2-17-21-22-24-25	9-23-26-27
December	1-10-17-21-22-23-26-27	24-25-31

2007 PLANTING GUIDE

	Aboveground Crops	Root Crops
January	3-21-22-26-30-31	3-10-11-12-13-17-18
February	18-22-23-26-27	6-7-8-9-14
March	21-22-25-26	5-6-7-8-9-13-14-18
April	1-18-22-23-29-30	2-3-4-5-9-10-14
May	1-19-20-26-27-28-29-30	1-2-11-12-15-16
June	15-16-22-23-24-25-26	3-4-7-8-11-12-30
July	20-21-22-23-28	3-4-9-12-14
August	16-17-18-19-24-25	1-5-6-10-28-29
September	12-13-14-15-16-20-21-25	2-5-6-29
October	12-13-18-22-23	3-10-26-27-30-31
November	14-15-18-19-22-23	7-8-9-26-27
December	11-12-16-20	4-5-6-7-24-25-30

	Pruning	Weeds and Pests
January	3-12-13	6-7-8-15-16
February	9-10	2-3-4-11-16
March	8-17-18	4-10-11-15-16
April	4-5-14	7-8-12-16
May	2-11-12	4-5-9-13-14
June	7-8	5-6-9-10-14
July	4-5-13-14	2-3-7-11-12-30
August	10-29	3-7-8-12-30-31
September	5-6	3-4-8-9-10-11-27
October	2-3-30-31	1-5-6-7-8-28-29
November	9-26-27	1-2-3-4-25-29-30
December	6-7-24-25	1-2-9-26-27-28-29

2007 PHASES OF THE MOON—
NEW YORK TIME

New Moon	First Quarter	Full Moon	Last Quarter
Dec. 20 ('06)	Dec. 27 ('06)	Jan. 3	Jan. 11
Jan. 18	Jan. 25	Feb. 2	Feb. 10
Feb. 17	Feb. 24	March 3	March 11
March 18	March 25	April 2	April 10
April 17	April 24	May 2	May 9
May 16	May 23	May 31	June 8
June 14	June 22	June 30	July 7
July 14	July 22	July 29	August 5
August 12	August 20	August 28	Sept. 3
Sept. 11	Sept. 19	Sept. 26	Oct. 3
Oct. 11	Oct. 19	Oct. 26	Nov. 1
Nov. 9	Nov. 17	Nov. 24	Dec. 1
Dec. 9	Dec. 17	Dec. 23	Dec. 31

Each phase of the Moon lasts approximately seven to eight days, during which the Moon's shape gradually changes as it comes out of one phase and goes into the next.

There will be a solar eclipse during the New Moon phase on March 18 and September 11.

There will be a lunar eclipse during the Full Moon phase on March 3 and August 28.

Use the Moon phases to connect you with your lucky numbers for this year. See the next page (page 112) and your lucky numbers.

LUCKY NUMBERS
FOR SCORPIO: 2007

Lucky numbers and astrology can be linked through the movements of the Moon. Each phase of the thirteen Moon cycles vibrates with a sequence of numbers for your Sign of the Zodiac over the course of the year. Using your lucky numbers is a fun system that connects you with tradition.

New Moon	First Quarter	Full Moon	Last Quarter
Dec. 20 ('06)	Dec. 27 ('06)	Jan. 3	Jan. 11
7 4 6 1	0 4 5 8	8 7 2 4	4 8 3 9
Jan. 18	Jan. 25	Feb. 2	Feb. 10
9 6 6 9	9 1 0 4	8 7 9 4	0 8 5 2
Feb. 17	Feb. 24	March 3	March 11
2 6 3 4	7 6 6 1	3 3 0 7	2 8 5 9
March 18	March 25	April 2	April 10
9 3 6 9	8 8 3 5	5 0 4 1	1 7 2 5
April 17	April 24	May 2	May 9
5 6 9 5	5 9 2 6	0 1 7 4	4 8 2 3
May 16	May 23	May 31	June 8
3 6 5 4	8 1 5 9	4 6 3 7	7 1 2 5
June 14	June 22	June 30	July 7
5 4 4 8	1 7 0 6	1 9 4 7	7 8 2 1
July 14	July 22	July 29	August 5
0 1 5 7	0 5 2 8	7 3 6 7	7 1 0 9
August 12	August 20	August 28	Sept. 3
9 4 6 1	0 5 6 3	2 1 2 5	5 4 4 8
Sept. 11	Sept. 19	Sept. 26	Oct. 3
8 1 0 5	9 6 3 8	5 3 6 5	5 5 9 2
Oct. 11	Oct. 19	Oct. 26	Nov. 1
2 0 1 7	7 4 8 5	6 9 8 8	8 3 5 0
Nov. 9	Nov. 17	Nov. 24	Dec. 1
0 4 1 7	7 2 5 9	9 2 2 6	6 8 0 7
Dec. 9	Dec. 17	Dec. 23	Dec. 31
7 4 1 5	5 8 9 8	8 7 7 2	4 0 8 3

SCORPIO
YEARLY FORECAST 2007

Forecast for 2007 Concerning Business
Prospects, Financial Affairs, Health,
Travel, Employment, Love and Marriage
for Persons Born with the Sun
in the Zodiacal Sign of Scorpio,
October 23–November 22.

For those born under the influence of the Sun in the zodiacal sign of Scorpio, ruled by Mars, planet of drive and
desire, and by Pluto, planet of transformative renewal,
this can be the year that takes you to the top of whatever ambitious mountain you've been climbing. Once
you've reached the pinnacle, deserved rewards will follow. Of major note in 2007 is the positive connection of
Saturn in Leo and Pluto in Sagittarius. A depth of commitment, unstoppable courage, and boundless enthusiasm can be gifts. But you may have to dig deep to
uncover such treasure. Remember, all that glitters is not
gold. So perceiving the essence of things beneath the
surface will be crucial. Also of note is Saturn's move to
Virgo in early September. Saturn in Virgo until the end
of 2009 and into 2010 highlights your sector of friendship, teamwork, and strategies. Set your sights on far
horizons for future accomplishments. As the year unfolds, keep a level head and a modest lifestyle to stay on
the straight and narrow where good health resides.
You'll have the resources for major travel adventures,
but will you have the time? Employment prospects
have never looked better. Chances of promotion, recog-

nition, and public success are more likely this year than in most others. Romance is an exciting dance that pulses on and off with rhythmic waves.

The first half of 2007 is a solid and promising stage for business, as Jupiter and Saturn are in cooperation. Take advantage of this opportune period. Growth can take off, and bigger and better things are to be expected. Don't fear the responsibility and commitment that inevitably come with worldly success. Learn to be modest about your accomplishments, but don't be shy to demonstrate and promote what you've achieved so far. This will give others, whether individuals or corporations, the confidence to back your ventures.

The first half of this year should set the tone in business for what follows, so read the signs that inform you of the state of play. At the start of March and the end of June, faith and integrity could be sorely tested. That means trust only those you must, as deception is possible by those whose ethical standards do not match yours. Rather than seeking revenge for betrayal or deceit, don't let anyone get away with it in the first place. Older and experienced players might have an edge in the commercial environment, especially those who have been preparing solidly for several years. Traditional enterprises will probably fare quite well. Technology can be temperamental in January, May, and October. So don't roll out the latest cutting-edge solutions at the wrong time. Make a clear decision about a plan or direction to follow in April, then check its progress by December. At that time some grand opportunity might be yours for the taking, whether it is earned by hard work or simply falls into your lap. However it comes, recognize what it is for you and go for it!

All this extraordinary potential depends on how you handle money and what status you've attained. The beneficial influence of Jupiter in Sagittarius is most likely experienced in your financial affairs. However much cash you have and earn, this is the ideal year to make money work for you rather than you always working for it. If you manage to accomplish this act of material magic by the end of 2007, when Jupiter finally connects with Pluto, you've accomplished a most important mission. By Christmas you should be like the king or queen in the counting house, relishing your prosperity and generously bestowing some of it on loved ones, friends, and valued associates.

Scorpios generally enjoy a mystery which needs to be unraveled through persistent investigation and sharp intuition. Your own health and well-being may the mystery for you to decode this year. With both Neptune and Chiron in Aquarius opposing Saturn in Leo until September, do not neglect physical needs. However strong you are, remind yourself of the frailty of even the strongest individuals. Immune system deficiency may be the underlying issue in any illness. Vulnerability can be significantly lessened with preventive care such as tonics, specific diets, and a healthy sustainable lifestyle. You may be paying the price for excessive or indulgent behavior last year. Drugs of all kinds are contraindicated for many sensitive Scorpios. Susceptibility to infection is heightened if you become run-down. Failing to live up to unreal expectations could be physically and mentally depressing, which won't help to sustain your well-being. Be cautious and self-protective when traveling, especially when your planetary ruler Mars retrogrades in Cancer during November and December. This is a possible time of physical stress if you have been reckless or thoughtless about your body's needs. There can be symptoms of low energy, chronic fatigue, depression, addiction, or hard-to-diagnose ailments. May through September is the important period to work positively with healers and healing regimens which in many cases can lead to miraculous recovery.

Getting away from it all may be a major theme, with exotic faraway destinations the lure. Late May into early June can be a fine juncture to take off. If you can't make it then, postpone travel until the second week of July. Head for places that offer the best swimming, surfing, diving, sailing, and fishing, all relaxing delights for water sign Scorpio. An island resort with sun, sea, and sand is just the tonic for urban Scorpios essentially indoors all year. Those of you with families should include the kids on at least one memorable vacation. If possible, make a unique journey with your lover to recapture the initial excitement of your relationship. Or run off with a playmate to escape the rat race as well as judgmental prying eyes. You will have the impulse and desire to put distance between yourself and your routine at times. A personal pilgrimage or a significant journey related to your job can emerge in your birthday period. But don't be too surprised if departure is delayed or if your sojourn away is longer than expected, possibly even into 2008. Once Jupiter arrives in Capricorn at year's end, shorter trips and domestic travel should become easier. Camping trips, outdoor adventures, or a tour of cultural landmarks and icons may have to wait until 2008.

The only limits to outstanding career potential and actual achievement are likely to be your own expectations and determination. Reach for the plum jobs at the top of your profession, trade, or occupation. However, it's likely that the most favorable opportunities and results flow to Scorpios in traditional and conservative occupations, as well as those of you with above average entrepreneurial skills. Work energetically and diligently in May and June to impress customers and management alike. This is also the best time for Scorpio job seekers to put your best foot forward and apply for better positions. Once an income peak is reached, possibly by the end of summer, attention will turn to vocational satisfaction and the less material dimensions of any position, such as status and recognition, power and authority.

Fancy-free Scorpio singles can have a ball, hooking up with interested and attractive partners. Spontaneous encounters can blossom and bear fruit as early as March and April. Then someone of significance can land in your life, seemingly out of nowhere. Be alert for any and all opportunities to meet that special someone. Whether love stays or not will be the question that's unanswerable until the moment arrives. Don't build a wall around yourself with preconceptions of what can happen in relationships. Scorpios who have been dating for a considerable period, and know who and what you want, may decide to tie the knot midyear. It should be a happy event that is widely and publicly celebrated. Couples could be concerned with issues of parenting or having kids. The eclipse pattern this year brings enormous emphasis to your horoscope sector of children. Give this instinctual arena the attention it deserves, working through challenges while accepting what destiny delivers to your door.

SCORPIO
DAILY FORECAST: 2007

1st Week/January 1–7

Monday January 1st. The mercurial energy of this first day of the new year should suit no-nonsense Scorpio who likes to tell it like it is. Sharp words exchanged at close quarters offer a chance for direct communication. Once you've made your position clear, move on and don't linger in analysis or regret. Domestic peace and calm will settle in the aftermath.

Tuesday the 2nd. Someone close may have issues with your style. Possibly they resent the power and control you exert over them. Collaborations at work or with financial projects could be stretched. Rather than pushing things to a potential breaking point, look out into the wider world for greater perspective and allow situations to settle.

Wednesday the 3rd. Today's Cancer Full Moon suits sensitive, intuitive Scorpio temperaments. It's a great day for special journeys, peppered with excitement and the unexpected. Meeting fun new people seems destined. They may become fine friends, stimulating companions, or even lovers. Pleasure in worldly, cultural activities makes this day anything but boring.

Thursday the 4th. Despite a growing and obvious need to take care of business and career, you probably have little interest in making money today. Perhaps a genuine ambition for higher learning has taken root, and you are captivated by prospects of greater expertise and knowledge. The lure of the foreign or an engagement with a distant figure could be a central distraction.

Friday the 5th. Drop recreational pursuits and throw yourself enthusiastically into earning a living. Performing on the job with flair and style puts you in the limelight for recognition and acknowledgment. Your reputation is heading in a positive direction. Motivated by the needs and support of those at home, grasp opportunities and make the most of them.

Saturday the 6th. Don't waste this day on trivial pursuits or pointless distraction. Discipline and determination will impel you to great effort in advancing your career or embarking on a commercial venture. Your endeavors make success and profitability almost certain. Major purchases you have researched and thoroughly considered can be made with confidence.

Sunday the 7th. Spending some of that hard-earned cash on social activities and outings will be easy. And you likely deserve a good time, even if it costs a little more. Spontaneity reigns, especially later in the day. So stay loose. Parents may be preoccupied with entertaining kids and their pals. Gatherings of recreational clubs hold a surprise.

Weekly Summary

A shakedown of personnel and social connections could rattle you as 2007 gets under way. There is certainly an edge to encounters, which Mars-ruled Scorpios may relish. No doubt you won't be inclined to back down from confrontation or disputes. But neither should you go out of your way looking for trouble or persist in behaving with insensitivity. Allies could become enemies through heavy-handedness. Be open to explanations from others who may have good reasons for their recent behavior. Nevertheless, once you're through with someone, be clear about it. Start the year with a clean slate and without looking back.

When Venus enters Aquarius midweek, the tone of your personal life can take a turn for the better. Perhaps it's about spending more time at home with loved ones or giving greater attention to refurbishing of your home. But getting your own way with those around you seems out of the question. Be alert to important communications.

2nd Week/January 8–14

Monday the 8th. Clear thinking can be a hallmark of proceedings, making this a great day for communicating any significant message or information. Every meeting or call can be brief yet effective. One individual, perhaps a sibling or neighbor, seems determined to get in touch for a discussion. Career advice from an experienced older person could prove invaluable.

Tuesday the 9th. Financial wrangling might throw a monkey wrench in the works. Payment for goods or services could be in dispute, and you will need to push for what is owed you. Buyers are in a mood for serious bargains and tough negotiations; selling them will be a challenge for you. Don't be tempted to sell your product or service short.

Wednesday the 10th. Sweet dreams are made of days like this. Time out with a loving partner beckons irresistibly. Other matters can wait. Your affectionate expressions will heal any wounds and offer a chance for togetherness. If a family member is unwell and needs your care, make their comfort your priority.

Thursday the 11th. Thinking too hard and long about perplexing problems is unlikely to resolve anything. It's sensible to try to understand a situation, but no amount of premeditation substitutes for action. Set appropriate limits to planning and strategy so that your safety and security are assured. Approval for what you want may not be forthcoming from those in authority.

Friday the 12th. Headstrong, selfish behavior will incur the disapproval of those who share your life. You may be too insistent on your own agenda, to the point of antagonizing or hasting others. Alternately, a playful mood might not mesh with the current domestic atmosphere. Get out for fun instead of upsetting the applecart at home. Reckless dating is sure to receive family criticism.

Saturday the 13th. You're in your element today with the Moon in Scorpio, but that doesn't mean taking things for granted. Intriguing, attractive individuals can prove slippery. Elusive characters may be untrustworthy, not what they seem. Perhaps you are attempting to fool yourself or others. Contact is easy. But trust, integrity, and security might be harder to come by.

Sunday the 14th. Career initiatives seem to be building to a head of steam. But launching action too soon would be counterproductive. Precise planning, even in the latter stages of a project, might make all the difference to success. Deep thought can be insightful and fruitful, lending clarity and form to what has been clouded and nebulous.

Weekly Summary

Initiative and enterprise will undoubtedly be well rewarded and suitably acknowledged during the week. This is the wrong time to hide your light under a bushel or indulge in false humility. You're onto something solid and of definite value in your profession, craft, or trade. Let the world know and see these capabilities and strengths.

Some Scorpios may have reached a pinnacle of mastery that deserves respect and recognition. Others appear determined and equipped to jump-start a pioneering endeavor whatever it takes. However, you still have to convince people who hold alternative views or iron out technical bugs.

Midweek serves as a reminder that damage can be done to the delicate fabric of personal and family relationships. You may be so obsessed with your own purposes that loved ones feel neglected. Someone's need for care and affection may become a turnoff. At the very least it will test your devotion and compassion. Either way, love sometimes hurts but also heals.

3rd Week/January 15–21

Monday the 15th. Acting like the last of the big spenders could be a danger to savings plans and budgets. The spontaneous impulse to splash out on an extravagant purchase might seem out of character, taking you by surprise. Make sure the item is needed as well as something you really want. Speculating with earnings, or trying to turn gambling into a steady income, is fraught with risk.

Tuesday the 16th. If finances have been unreliable or inconsistent, now is the time to assess the situation and do something to make a real difference. Establishing economic security is paramount. If you're already on track, making a big push to increase your cash flow can be spectacularly successful. This is not an overnight success, but the fruitful results of long determination.

Wednesday the 17th. Scorpios are strengthened to say what you think directly, without beating about the bush.

Yet you have the flexibility to try alternate ways and diverse approaches if objectives aren't accomplished or communication is resisted. Calls, correspondence, and conversation are clearly informative and offer unequivocal direction. You'll know where you stand.

Thursday the 18th. Noteworthy ideas and concepts may form and crystallize, likely related to career ambitions or worldly progress. Addressing authorities is favored, as long as you're not expecting an immediate response. You will be considered in their good time. The seed of an educational or travel decision can prompt definite action and commitment in the month ahead.

Friday the 19th. The overnight New Moon kicks off a fresh lunar month. Finish up affairs that may involve short journeys and communicative connections. Then give the domestic front deserved attention. Home improvement ideas can be researched and applied. Novel concepts of architecture, living design, and feng shui will appeal to you.

Saturday the 20th. A cluster of planets in Aquarius can cause discomfort in many Scorpio households. Understanding that you're not always the center of attention is a key to awareness as those you live with assert themselves and make themselves heard. Commitment to love and devotion might mean sacrifices in other areas. A long-held personal dream could manifest for true believers.

Sunday the 21st. An active, playful day suits you. Recreation should be fun and healthy. Start early, hopefully with a focus on physical exertion and challenge. Sport and games or pastimes and hobbies that require practical application of artfulness would be ideal. Parents will enjoy exuberant children. Lovers are infused with lusty desire.

Weekly Summary

Three planets change from Capricorn to Aquarius during this period. The energy of the Aquarius New Moon blows fresh winds. Strategies need to change with newly emerging circumstances. Many Scorpios should consider the quality of satisfaction within the arena of private life. Family and home take on huge significance temporarily. They provide the foundation and underpinning of all outer aspirations and accomplishment.

Establishing yourself in a new living situation might be the overall task for some of you. Others will want to rearrange the furniture or redecorate the apartment to enliven and refresh the space. Receiving guests and visiting relatives can make this a period when the house is full to overflowing. Shared households may be sadly saying good-bye to certain members and considering new ones.

Special experiences of love can mark this period with true romance. However, there's little room for rose-colored glasses. Efforts at refining communication help heal relationship rifts and family feuds.

4th Week/January 22–28

Monday the 22nd. Chaos is a leading indicator of a potential creative breakthrough, so don't resist inevitable change. Some people you relate to now could seem frenzied and unreliable. Offer a steady helping hand. Be part of the solution rather than another problem for them. Pleasures, pastimes, and children can all be sources of unexpected expense. No doubt you will err on the side of generosity.

Tuesday the 23rd. Your ruling planet Mars in Capricorn, a sign of its strength, signals a fine opportunity to develop and enhance personal vigor. It may be both emotional and mental, but you should not neglect the physical. Working hard is no substitute for exercise. Don't let your stamina slip. Instead, the challenge is to become even more fit and healthy, which should bolster every undertaking.

Wednesday the 24th. Hard work pays off now, so give it everything you've got, and then some! The boss should notice any extra effort and consider you for a bonus or promotion. Satisfied customers will sing your praises and help to build further business. Inspiration and perspiration combine to great effect. Finally, the demands of career and personal life can be brought into healthy balance.

Thursday the 25th. Expect some friction on the domestic front. Whether it's trouble in paradise or simply the usual household disputes, give any antagonists the respect they deserve and hear them out. Loving someone doesn't imply always being in agreement and harmony. Healthy relationships are able to tolerate, acknowledge, and contain individual differences and personal preferences.

Friday the 26th. Someone you love or respect is simply not on the same page as you today. They may be unable to share a vision or concept that seems clear and obvious to you. Maybe there's a misunderstanding caused by inadequate communication. Try to make your point again at some other time. But it's possible they just won't ever get it, however inspired it seems.

Saturday the 27th. Pleasing a partner could be too hard. Perhaps you don't understand what they want. Or if you do, you don't agree with it or possibly even care. Open discussion later should clear the air and renew mutual appreciation. Doors to trust and intimacy open only when differences are confronted. Visiting the family may not be wise. Someone may have a bone to pick or a criticism to make.

Sunday the 28th. Changes are in the air, likely to be positive. Generosity of spirit and an accepting attitude will help the exchange of serious, even shocking matters. Yet facts are facts, no matter how unlikely or unexpected. Don't dismiss or make light of what seems crucial to others. A relationship could be suddenly on or off but certainly won't be the same.

Weekly Summary

Someone could be promoting wild schemes or taking crazy risks. Strange things can happen, even without anyone intending it. Maintain a healthy distrust of technology gurus and financial wizards, as they might be incompetent or untrustworthy. Also restrain reckless behavior on your part. Gamblers could be heading for a fall. So if you're ahead, take the money and run. If not, cut your losses. Casual dating appears expensive, so be cautious about what you propose. With wild cards in the deck, many Scorpio players will act with greater caution and reserve. Tend investments and business with astute care, keeping financial deals to yourself. Protect your personal affairs from invasive characters and prying eyes.

A clarity of vision should steer you straight if you're awake and aware. Late in the week Venus enters Pisces, heralding a period of art, love, and beauty for sensitive, receptive, intuitive Scorpios.

5th Week/January 29–February 4

Monday the 29th. Money matters today, and Scorpios keeping detailed, accurate records are well placed. If you've neglected maintaining order with financial statements and records, get organized now. Call on the help of a professional where complex, critical business is involved. You will have affairs in hand so that loans for property and commercial expansion can be seriously considered.

Tuesday the 30th. A mental contest with a clever individual can test your wits. In legal affairs, you can gain the upper hand, but only if you know your rights or your lawyer knows his stuff. Intellectual puzzles or games present the sort of challenge that suits your active mind. Smart solutions are possible but only after directly wrestling with any problem.

Wednesday the 31st. Interests, people, and places that are far removed could capture your attention, whether relevant or not. Feeding a yearning for exotic experiences provides a welcome distraction from humdrum activity. Higher studies in intriguing areas of knowledge or explorations of future travel plans may be emotionally satisfying. But be aware that little work will be done as a consequence.

Thursday February 1st. Anticipation builds through the day, leading to the Full Moon forming after midnight tonight. Career and professional matters are in the spotlight. It's time to perform, displaying what you've learned and mastered. Put your best foot forward to promote business or to get a chance at the top job. A cheering squad at home backs you all the way. Parents need attention now.

Friday the 2nd. In any endeavor now, a bird in the hand will be worth two in the bush. Stick to the straight and narrow. Then you're guaranteed to arrive at your destination or achieve a desired goal. Putting ambitions in the too-hard basket, while losing yourself in a private fantasyland, seems a cop out. The opportunity for success is too good to miss and merely awaits determined effort.

Saturday the 3rd. Diversity of opinion keeps any group or organization lively and responsive. Expect to have your views countered by other intelligent and articulate individuals. Listen and learn rather than react defensively. Team sports and recreational clubs offer engaging interactions and activities. Take part as a dynamic, expressive member with unique qualities to offer a group.

Sunday the 4th. An unusual adventure is what many Scorpios will seek today. Novel or untried challenges should be heaps of fun. A sense of daring or a wild buddy might urge you to take a physical risk just for the buzz. Maybe it's some extreme sport. Whatever the choice, make sure it's not boring because it's all about the adrenaline rush.

Weekly Summary

The Sun's annual hookup with Chiron takes place in Capricorn, your sector of home and family, roots, and real estate, at the very foundations of your private life. If all is well in this arena, rest assured and pour energy into other areas, such as commerce and career.

Yet a thorough, honest assessment might show care is needed here. Perhaps domestic relationships have deteriorated because of neglect or misunderstanding. Maybe a relative is ailing and needs your caring ministrations. Or property could be desperate for repairs and maintenance. Do what is needed on the domestic front, returning the situation to functional if not optimal health.

Midweek, put your money where your mouth is and then move on to more relaxing and pleasurable pastimes. Astute Scorpios can make money even while you play. Family or home-based businesses might become profitable, freeing up cash for fun and entertainment. Daring adventures beckon, likely encouraged by youngsters or a lover.

6th Week/February 5–11

Monday the 5th. Socializing can easily derail efforts at making a buck and getting the job done. Flirtations at the office would undermine your reputation in the company, as would casualness with customers. Understand where your interests lie and put in a fair day's work for a fair day's pay. Spending may prove unsatisfying or annoying. Settle for fun that is free.

Tuesday the 6th. High anticipation and excitement, perhaps around a creative project or love affair, make it harder than usual to relax. Even in the midst of busy periods, rest and relieving stress remain essential for your well-being. Are you running life from a calm command center? Or are external pressures and agendas running you? Check within yourself for the answer.

Wednesday the 7th. Extraordinary inspiration and imaginative effort can have personally fulfilling and financially rewarding results. Practical considerations can temper your vision to good effect. Spare cash would be well spent on domestic refinements, implementing elegant design and style. A surge of loving appreciation might prompt a grand romantic gesture or gift.

Thursday the 8th. There may be time for a secret rendezvous or a background deal. After taking care of unfinished private business, the real fun starts with the Moon again in your sign. Expressing your feelings becomes easier, enhancing communication but leaving nowhere to hide. Fairy-tale outcomes may result for Scorpios who dare. But fear of embarrassment, exposure, or ridicule could hold you back.

Friday the 9th. Greeting the day with exuberant confidence is justified. Your luck is in and your intuition is on. A spontaneous joy might sweep you up with a sense that life is for the living, and it's all good. The Moon is still in your sign of Scorpio till evening. But before midnight the Moon enters Sagittarius, and everything can change. Deceptions may disappoint your expectations.

Saturday the 10th. Strength and self-discipline will be needed to handle recent obstacles or disillusionment. Mental toughness and a realistic appraisal of current circumstances should assist you in making decisions or determining a particular response. While there may be a bevy of invitations for social celebrations and fun activities, Scorpio could be in the mood to keep to yourself.

Sunday the 11th. Wild ideas and impulsive moves cost you now, so leave your credit cards in your wallet. If you're taking risks, make sure it's not with others' money. The pursuit of thrills can be expensive, especially if they involve the latest fads. Shopping for technology toys is one way to provide distraction and relieve boredom.

Weekly Summary

The early part of this week calls for time out in your own space. Take stock of what's been going down and what's coming up. Resist taunts and temptations to jump on someone's bandwagon. Stick to your own agenda. Turning the other cheek when offended is difficult for Scorpio. Yet compassion, forgiveness, and understanding offer the best course now.

A fresh burst of social enthusiasm arrives midweek. Stimulating, attractive companions are seeking your participation in their fun and games. Singles can easily hook up. Lovers will be ecstatic in the delight of each other. Children occupy parents in the best of ways. At least for a little while, living the ideal dream is a real possibility. Those of you without expectations will fare best by being in the moment and contributing to the happiness of others.

Caution and consequences finally kick in, raining on certain parades. A fork in the road appears. Even if you're emotionally vulnerable, don't make matters worse by being financially foolish as well.

7th Week/February 12–18

Monday the 12th. A dose of optimism is a good tonic for emotionally sensitive Scorpio. This is true if you've been burdened by self-doubt, disillusionment, or guilt. Intuition can be finely honed now and useful as a tool in commercial affairs. Whether you're an artist trying to succeed in business or a creative entrepreneur, making a profit entails taking a risk.

Tuesday the 13th. Greater career success might rest upon improving your educational qualifications. Think through a plan of action to enhance knowledge and skills. Information management is more than a concept. It's a way of life in the digital age. Step one is to bring structured order to this arena. Then you can find what you need and assess whether you're making progress in reaching your goals.

Wednesday the 14th. Focused energy should serve you well. Speaking and corresponding can be impressive because of your confidence and certain knowledge about the subject. Solid conviction is certainly influential in swinging people to your view. Learning more about a favorite subject is a joy. Expect at least one Valentine's Day card that affirms committed love.

Thursday the 15th. An exercise program or gym routine is a priority now. Even if you have more important matters to attend to, letting physical maintenance and preventive health measures slip is not an option. Leaving work early or generally staying close to home will suit you. This dark Moon phase is ideal for completing duties and then getting an early night with deep sleep.

Friday the 16th. A time of reckoning is approaching. Personal hopes and aspirations will be tested in the crucible of external reality. A particular project, or an overall way of life, is either feasible or not. What can't be sustained in the real world should now cease in favor of what is working. One way to measure this is by honestly examining the financial bottom line.

Saturday the 17th. Today's New Moon suggests that you get organized for the month ahead. Deal with household shopping and paying bills during the course of the day. Then the evening will be free for relaxation and pleasure. Family and private life can come into meaningful focus. A meeting of the clan over a shared meal will promote a secure sense of belonging.

Sunday the 18th. If the last few days have been quiet and dutiful, you're in for a pleasant surprise. Stimulation and excitement are guaranteed, in great company too! Parents find kids a lively if enjoyable handful. An adventurous outing may be necessary to express high spirits. Scorpio singles fare well in spontaneous encounters, with attractive players eager to hook up.

Weekly Summary

Taking care of business is the best way to start this week. That might mean curtailing certain indulgent pleasures and distracting pastimes. Look closely at household needs when making a budget or as an incentive to making money.

Venus and Mars are in harmony, promoting pleasing social exchanges and activating creative projects. Education for enjoyment as well as for a purpose is favored and should prove satisfying if you apply yourself. Low-key flirtations infiltrate even humdrum situations, whetting the appetite of amorous Scorpios.

One challenge in the current astrological landscape is the start of a retrograde Mercury. This planet of travel, communication, and commerce will spend the next two weeks going retrograde in Pisces. Rethinking some ideas and revisiting some pleasures could be part of this reflective period. Children require close attention, as do love affairs and speculative financial ventures. Artists are well served with an opportunity to review creative projects, making changes to refine the work.

8th Week/February 19–25

Monday the 19th. Envy or jealousy may creep into even the most beautiful affairs. Trying to keep a tight grip to sustain happy circumstances will squeeze the joy out of them. Guard against controlling or manipulating loved ones, as that would only breed resentment. Allow a flow of experience to sweep you up rather than strategically forcing outcomes you think you want.

Tuesday the 20th. Work hard today, and rewards are sure to follow. Definite goals and energetic confidence will ensure success in both big and small undertakings. Be glad to have a demanding occupation or a challenge to tackle, then get on with the job. If you're seeking new employment or a better position, throw your hat into the ring with self-assurance. You do possess the necessary skills and experience.

Wednesday the 21st. When the going gets tough, tough Scorpios get going. Expect obstacles and tests to arise. However, they're likely just blips in what can unfold as a period of major career and financial achievement. If things were always easy, there would be no pride in accomplishment. Minor irritations like traffic jams or rude customers shouldn't cloud the bigger positive picture.

Thursday the 22nd. Living at close quarters with your partner, a relative, or a roommate could be wearing thin. Changes may be needed to alleviate crowding or interference. Perhaps a different apartment is the answer. Or maybe living together is simply not the right thing any longer. Family affairs and pressures could be negatively impacting your relationship. Be patient and flexible.

Friday the 23rd. Physically fit Scorpios will enjoy working out today with good companions who enjoy sharing the experience. Those of you who are lazier or less aerobically inclined would definitely benefit from the positive guidance and motivation of a coach or personal trainer. Conversational complications can set in later. Watch for pointless arguments or careless verbal blunders, especially with loved ones.

Saturday the 24th. The first quarter Moon forms in Gemini before dawn, starting a phase that can be tense. Kids, money, and relationships seem chaotic and possibly troublesome. Keep plans, arrangements, and activities simple in order to avoid confusion. Miscommunication could derail finely tuned schedules. Listen closely while reading between the lines.

Sunday the 25th. The morning is excellent for mending fences and rebuilding bridges in partnerships or with household members. Lovers might indulge in some early sweet romance. Differences dissolve with genuine care and mutual appreciation. Leave money out of the equation. Recreational pastimes and creative pursuits beckon more loudly than the mall.

Weekly Summary

A feisty start to the week puts many Scorpios on defensive toes. Offense may be taken where it's not intended. Be as sensitive to others' feelings as you can be about your own. Obsession is a Scorpio trait, and you may be in the grip of a compelling interest or person. A need to achieve could sweep you up in a passionate frenzy. With both the Moon and Venus in fiery Aries, impulse might lead to doing things over or regretfully stepping on the wrong toes.

Midweek Mercury retrograde in Pisces is conjunct with the Pisces Sun. Logic and rationality give way to imaginings and apprehension. Mental processes are neither strong nor clear. Meticulous tasks requiring sharp thinking are better left alone. Still, this can be a period of incredible imagination and profound intuitive awareness. Applying it to the real world will prove harder.

Late in the week, do your best to complete correspondence and formal documents. Students should make every effort to finish assignments and assure that required reading is done. Keep the atmosphere at home centered and calm.

9th Week/February 26–March 4

Monday the 26th. Craft skills and decorative flair come in handy around the house. Maybe it's time to add an exotic touch to the decor. Learning more to further a hobby comes easily, with references and teachers on hand. You may share activities and interests you love with the wider world, perhaps by promoting or lecturing. A pleasurable outing unfolds for the curious and adventurous Scorpio.

Tuesday the 27th. Technical problems readily find creative solutions now, but they will still take time to implement. Exciting new ideas and fresh information need to be digested until they're thoroughly understood. Scorpio travelers may feel sure of the way when revisiting familiar places. Yet it's still possible to get lost, perhaps delightfully so! A guide could appear in the nick of time.

Wednesday the 28th. A colleague might openly oppose your way of doing things. Perhaps all you can do is refer any dispute to the boss. Unfortunately, things may not go all your way, but it will be too late to back down. An amicable outcome is possible if you value working together. This is a great chance to put your cards on the table.

Thursday March 1st. Scorpio entrepreneurs could see results and reap rewards from a combination of hard work and seizing opportunities as they arise. It's about doing both, not just one or the other. Having a vision of ideal outcomes and a positive intention to succeed also greatly helps to make things happen. Show what you're capable of by achieving rather than talking about it.

Friday the 2nd. Many Scorpios can be on a roll making money. Whether it's from a business, professional career, or investment decisions, take care to preserve what you earn. Foolish risk, carelessness, or laziness might result in loss through an easy come, easy go attitude. Self-doubt, inner questioning, and second-guessing will paralyze effective action. Stick to a clear plan.

Saturday the 3rd. It's very important to loosen up and take a break from the weight of worldly concerns. Spontaneous invitations to social gatherings and parties should prove both entertaining and revitalizing. Today's Full Moon and lunar eclipse can bring a sense of vibrant celebration in good company. Take advantage of unexpected pleasures. Enjoy genuine time-out.

Sunday the 4th. Past associations could arouse unpleasant feelings or difficult memories. Unfinished family business may need sorting out. This probably takes time. It's best to make a start rather than put things off. Family members seem in a mood to discuss deep, personal issues. By listening attentively, you'll learn much even if it's not all upbeat and rosy.

Weekly Summary

Perplexing issues may arise, as Mercury continues its retrograde passage in Aquarius. Use your intuition. Tune in to where relatives or those with whom you live are really at. You'll be busy at work as well. But take care of matters at home, or there can be unsettling consequences to the stability of relationships.

This is no time to shelve problems in the too-hard basket. Do not bury your head in the sand, using business and the job as an excuse. The right solutions will present themselves if you make genuine attempts to find them. Resolutions may well come from others, so be open to intelligent input even if you don't immediately see eye-to-eye.

It's certainly a period of serious and profound consideration about where your life is heading and whether or not you're making headway. Even amid such heavy going, lightening up is essential to balance things out and keep all in perspective. Party and play when the need and opportunity arise. This will help in healing relationships and in finding answers.

10th Week/March 5–11

Monday the 5th. Private purposes take priority now, and they likely require undisturbed time for focus and inspiration. Working alone today should be highly productive. A sense of urgency and motivation will power any initiatives. There is great satisfaction in finally getting around to unfinished business and overdue tasks. Once things are done, relax and unwind.

Tuesday the 6th. Never underestimate the special fulfillment that comes from being in the right job. Appreciate the level and quality of recent success and achievement. Bask in the warm inner glow of missions accomplished. Don't take things for granted. Do continue with industrious effort. Yet it's important to taste the quality of life you've been working so hard to establish.

Wednesday the 7th. A period of meditation or thoughtful contemplation might reveal important ideas and solutions from the depths of your unconscious. You've probably been working on issues in the background. Now the results of that process can come to light. Planning financial moves or changing living arrangements is favored as long as you heed your own inner voice.

Thursday the 8th. Self-assertion comes easily now that the Moon is again in your sign. Yet it might prove too easy to slip into overdoing it. Try not to ride roughshod over others. It's really pointless and counterproductive. If you're looking for a fight, you'll find one. Having an ax to grind or losing your temper may have unpleasant consequences even though you're just trying to be open and honest about your feelings.

Friday the 9th. Disaffection may continue, especially with family or household members. Whether it's you or them, someone is not pleased. Both realists and dreamers can be disappointed when what had been hoped for fails to materialize as you expected. A fine solution is to be content with what is happening at the moment. Perhaps this is the definition of happiness.

Saturday the 10th. Shopping could preoccupy Scorpios with money burning a hole in your pocket. In any exchange, make sure you're buying treasure rather than trash. Beauty is generally in the eye of the beholder, but it would be better to end up with the ordinary rather than the fanciful. The sirens of fashion may distract you. You really need to purchase practical items such as hardware or groceries.

Sunday the 11th. Plans and dreams for a beautiful home could be taking shape. Rewards for working hard and sticking to a practical plan are leading to a better quality of life for you and yours. Any wobbles or setbacks are temporary. If you must do business, it should be profitable. Romantic, artistic, and spiritual dimensions of experience beckon free spirits.

Weekly Summary

There's sure to be an irregular, even wild, start to this week. It's time for something completely different. Getting away from the regular routines will do you a world of good. Try to be flexible about schedules and commitments so that you can be spontaneous. Having fun doing your own thing is likely to appeal. And you never know who you'll meet in the process.

Midweek Mercury finally grinds into forward gear again, signifying improvement in travel, transportation, and communications. Agreements and contracts can now proceed. Broken machinery and malfunctioning digital devices should respond to appropriate maintenance and repair. Domestic relationships are set to improve.

With Venus joining the harmony between Jupiter and Saturn, wonderful financial and career prospects could clearly emerge. Yet this is no time to foolishly push your luck or take things for granted. Best results come from confidently taking advantage of positive situations you've been working toward.

11th Week/March 12–18

Monday the 12th. Your special affinity with planet Pluto makes this a powerhouse of a day for go-getters. Ambitious Scorpio can tap a deep well of enthusiastic motivation. Even the biggest challenges can be tackled with relish and an expectation of success. Making a conscious effort to express loving devotion or erotic desire should evoke a suitably passionate response.

Tuesday the 13th. This is a time of solid achievement for Scorpio. Your accomplishments are likely built on a sense of order and structure in your daily affairs. This is a good day to give dutiful attention to organizing and filing correspondence, whether it's paper or digital. Check with the milestones and goals you have set to ensure that everything is on track.

Wednesday the 14th. A spontaneous sense of community in the neighborhood can bring you together with like-minded individuals who want to clean up and beautify the environment. Perhaps a wider program could be promoted, encouraging and inviting broad participation. Involvement with schools, politics, and civic affairs might mean neglecting your own chores for now.

Thursday the 15th. Staying at home can be very healing at present and may be essential for continued well-being and productivity. However, that doesn't mean lazing around and taking it easy. It should mean an opportunity to get housework under control while attending to the needs or demands of those around you. You're definitely in no mood for disagreements or criticism.

Friday the 16th. After a period of toil and dutiful effort, a relaxing break is in order. While business as usual may be your pattern, consider gifting yourself with a long weekend. Don't feel guilty if you pursue personal creativity and private responsibilities that meet the expectations of others. Exceptional inspiration strikes when it does and should be followed.

Saturday the 17th. Take advantage of a watery Moon in Pisces this weekend by letting yourself really unwind. Indulge whatever pleasures take your fancy, although overdoing it may be costly. Parents will enjoy the imaginative playfulness of youngsters. Singles can put out feelers for company in an easygoing, casual manner. It's best to avoid anything that is not fun.

Sunday the 18th. Tonight's approaching New Moon in Pisces could make this a crackerjack social day. Receptive, freewheeling Scorpios who are out for action won't be disappointed. Games, sports, crafts, and hobbies will be amusing, especially with others sharing similar interests. New pals stimulate and open you to unexplored territory.

Weekly Summary

Get business affairs under control and out of the way early in the week when you're most in the mood. You may encounter a dilemma between pursuing greater wealth or tasting a decent quality of life. Err on the side of health, whatever that means for you. Building blocks of enduring success are most likely already in place. So turn your attention now to physical needs and family well-being.

Open, honest, deeply thoughtful conversation is just what Scorpios appreciate. There should be plenty of that to whet your appetite midweek. One encounter could prove erotically attractive and deliciously desirable. Whether it's with your regular partner, a coworker, or someone recently met, it may prove irresistible.

Saturday night Venus enters Taurus, one of her favorite home zones. This can bring benefit and good times with a loving companion. But slow and steady wins this race. As the New Moon forms, secret liaisons can be indulged at a gradual pace. Let tension build while keeping your intentions under wraps a tad longer!

12th Week/March 19–25

Monday the 19th. The working week commences with the Moon in Aries, your work sector. Take advantage of a sense of duty to get things done. Cleaning, cooking, and chores on the domestic front can be effectively handled. Competitors in business may be testing your mettle, forcing your hand. Rise to the challenge. Watch for early signs of minor illness, possibly because of lowered immunity.

Tuesday the 20th. If you pushed yesterday to establish momentum, this can be a period of steady progress. Applying yourself on the job is to be preferred over seeking easy ways out and pleasurable distractions. Aspiring to a quality life, both for yourself and your family, helps propel action and effort in any undertaking. Help from others can be valuable and effective now.

Wednesday the 21st. For Scorpios, the spring equinox means getting down to work. But this doesn't mean simply working without any plan except survival. Check in with your spouse or lover for the reassurance that you're heading in the right direction. If in doubt, let them take the lead. Expressing affection and devotion can strengthen relationships. Love and romance may easily become the main game.

Thursday the 22nd. If you feel caught between a rock and a hard place, you're probably not alone. Perhaps it's a partner or someone close who is in difficult straits. Support those in need, but don't struggle with what can't be changed. Acceptance of reality and current conditions is essential. Yet some Scorpios will want to ignore or fudge the truth. Honesty is always the best policy.

Friday the 23rd. Contrary or varying opinions and approaches inevitably occur. It's how they're handled that makes all the difference. Your unique creativity may not be appreciated by others, even individuals you trust. Appreciate their perspective without being discouraged or overreacting. Mutual understanding only comes from openly talking things out while listening intelligently.

Saturday the 24th. Another's enthusiasm could feel overwhelming or disorienting. Taking on too much or trying to do everything at once is possibly misguided or ill-timed. Focus on one or two key objectives, then coordinate with a smart collaborator to accomplish them. Mistakes can be costly, but getting things just right will be profitable. Think clearly and act with precision.

Sunday the 25th. Tastes and styles can differ markedly today. Your idea of fun may not be shared by people you normally hang out with. If the kids or your lover want to do something you don't particularly like or enjoy, think twice before shooting it down. When planning activities, choose the creative, fun path. It's a leisure day, so skip the routine chores.

Weekly Summary

A wealth of dynamic energy waits to be harnessed. Once the Sun enters Aries Tuesday night, playtime is largely over and it's time to get down to work. Scorpio seeking to improve your occupational status should push in that direction. If you are truly motivated or in need, take on a second job that would increase your earnings. Partners and colleagues can display initiative and passion, which is infectious. Take their cue rather than resisting or going it alone.

A major decision appears on the horizon midweek. It's likely an issue that can't be stalled, fudged, or faked. Steel yourself to make a commitment that is clear to all. If you can't, someone else might make it for you, whether you're ready or agreeable. This may involve career, property, family, or a relationship, but some situation needs to turn the corner.

Late in the week, scenarios soften and become more amenable to genuine agreement but not to compromise or neglect. A special romantic, creative, or spiritual experience awaits sensitive individuals of vision, dedication, and idealism.

13th Week/March 26–April 1

Monday the 26th. Exciting journeys, or at least the prospect of going somewhere special, make a vibrant start to the week. Learning about new people, places, and things refreshes your outlook on the future. Meetings and encounters prove surprising yet enjoyable. Performances, promotions, and public relations schemes are original and entertaining. Foreign connections proceed smoothly.

Tuesday the 27th. If you need to go anywhere today, make your move before lunch to ensure a timely, safe, hassle-free arrival at your destination. Business and career take priority later. You may be working later than you expected, albeit productively and to good effect. A relative might have the right connections to further your interests or introduce you to someone at the top.

Wednesday the 28th. Business as usual should be the mantra today, despite some distractions or obstacles. The unavoidable need to give full attention to a work situation may not please your partner, who wants quality time and affectionate attention. Take home a gift as a peace offering. For working parents, child care may become an issue.

Thursday the 29th. Unresolved tension could erupt into a full-blown argument or battle. Rivalry in the workplace might peak as competitors show their hands and make their moves. If management is behind you, there'll be no need to struggle or be defensive. Stick to your regular game plan, then•you can succeed and win. An unhappy man around the house might make domestic life edgy.

Friday the 30th. Heeding your gut instinct can be hard when you are confronted with opposing ideas that seem clever. If you can't make up your mind, talk things over with a friend or coworker whose opinion you value. Maybe it's not about choosing one way over another but is an intelligent blending of both. The best solutions and plans incorporate analysis with intuition.

Saturday the 31st. Life certainly won't be boring today, but it may be disruptive. Shelve rigid plans for this weekend. Instead, allow yourself to be swept up in a wave of spontaneity. Pals can call or visit out of the blue, forcing you to put aside your schedule. A club or team to which you belong could have its customs and rituals challenged by renegade members or financial pressures.

Sunday April 1st. Unexpected fun will fill many a Scorpio heart with excitement. You may get to know a new playmate, one who appears quite different from your usual peers. A novel form of recreation is there for you to enjoy. It can lead to new discoveries about greater possibilities. One hitch today might be about stretching the budget to remain reasonably solvent.

Weekly Summary

Jumping through the various hoops of regular life can be either comforting or unsettling. Taking care of business out in the world means having to deal with people in high positions and large organizations. Taking an authoritative stand could be required in order for you to assert your unique ethics. Doing so will garner respect for your position, but probably only after a few battles are waged and won.

Special points in time do appear, here and there, as oases of welcome respite. Try not to get caught up in a whirlwind of doings. Do try to embrace needed balance. A few Scorpios might not know what to do when it becomes really quiet. Busyness could be a gear you're stuck in.

Stop to smell the daisies when the chance presents itself. Turn off the ignition for a minute and just be. Stars of romance are strong and sparky on the weekend. Another's scintillating presence will be an absolute pleasure. Loving distractions wait in the wings. Kick up your heels, at least once.

14th Week/April 2–8

Monday the 2nd. Scorpio musicians and artists may show the right stuff. Auditions and performances can get results justifying any previous sweat and tears. Joining an orchestra, stage show, or other creative group will validate your natural ability. Hard work and charm are a potent mix right now. Hone your talents through disciplined practice.

Tuesday the 3rd. Money or a desired possession could loom large today. Coffers may be happily emptied and credit limits pushed. Conversely, there might be funds flowing in, too, and a decent amount at that. Either way, price can be no object when you truly value something that inspires you. Feel-good purchases are high on your agenda, but keep your spending in proportion.

Wednesday the 4th. Are you sure someone is not being viewed through rose-colored lenses, distorting the real relationship? Or perhaps someone has beguiled you by talking big and stretching the facts? It would pay to review what a person has said, then ask yourself what they actually meant. The bottom line is that the truth is hard to discern right now, especially if desire is paramount.

Thursday the 5th. Intuitive hunches and psychic impressions are there for the perceiving. All water signs would do well to listen to that little voice within. Lucky breaks are likely in store for Scorpios trusting a gut feeling. Becoming torn between a responsibility and an urge to escape can inhibit any action at all. One thing may have to be surrendered if another is to be handled well.

Friday the 6th. Scorpio is a major sign of lessons learned through the dynamics of desire. Desire is switched on now. Rivalry and contest can also arise, especially when you are in pursuit of gratification. All could be fair in love and war, whether you like it or not. A love triangle demands that everyone put their cards on the table. Frankness will serve you better than evasiveness.

Saturday the 7th. Kissing and making up can be a predictable dance for some lovers. The sweetest of nothings count, along with thoughtful little touches. Giving or receiving a gift is possible. Why not say it with flowers? Dates should go exceptionally well even if there's a certain interruption. An older and respected figure, especially a patriarchal individual, demands attention.

Sunday the 8th. An indulgent tone may predominate to-day, especially in the early hours. Getting lost in many kinds of discussion and musing can become a pleasant pastime. Scorpio with little ones could have to prevent them from disrupting the peace. In contrast, the ambitious Scorpio with an eye on the career ball can work hard at getting ahead.

Weekly Summary

Anything or anyone trying to sabotage or undermine positive results could get caught in the spotlight of Monday's Full Moon in Libra. This could relate to others or to your own behavior. Whatever destructive tendencies are simmering under the surface will require some damage control. Shrugging off difficult issues or keeping your head buried in the sand will only compound any growing problem. The good thing is that if moves are made now, most circumstances can be righted.

Motivating Mars, Scorpio's coruling planet, is highlighted midweek in beautiful aspect to powerful Pluto, your ruling planet. This connects your domestic and financial sectors. Family might somehow prove of profound benefit. The clan may rally loyal support, aiding in great change. Dealings with major assets such as real estate can be memorable.

Important cosmic gears shift at the end of the week. Mars enters magical Pisces, and lovely Venus is receptive to a poetic Mercury. Dulcet melodies may be sung by a lover. Communicating is a pleasure to be shared and savored. Enjoy!

15th Week/April 9–15

Monday the 9th. Favorable fortune and beneficial breaks can visit you now. Scorpio beginners in various arenas are in for a special brand of luck. Helpful teachers, guides, and coaches come in many forms now, lending good support. The confidence to embark on learning a new skill should increase. An open regard and optimistic attitude will breed the best kind of success.

Tuesday the 10th. The smallest word is capable of generating strong responses, even if it's not apparent at first. A quip delivered in jest to a customer or colleague might be taken offensively. A loved one could also take something the wrong way. Remain aware that others have their own sensibilities and sensitivities, especially regarding what is of value. Quirky fun comes from a child.

Wednesday the 11th. Touching base with a family member will mean communicating by phone or e-mail, or possibly a visit in person. Even though traveling could feel irksome, it is definitely worth the journey. Spending quality time with a parent or mentor figure will reinforce a spiritual bonding. Compassionate motivation and inspired imagination make an uplifting blend.

Thursday the 12th. Authority and bureaucracy are likely to be on the heavy-handed side. When dealing with a large organization, play the game according to the rules and pull the right strings. Acquiescence rather than argument will go the longest way toward meeting an aim. Anyone who is tempted to bribe and manipulate will feel pleased. But sneaky tactics may lead to a no-win outcome.

Friday the 13th. The bond in an affiliation may not be as strong as supposed. Someone can be of two minds about making a particular commitment. Your personal resources might be drained more than those of a colleague. A shared endeavor could sour over the perception that a partnership is somehow unequal. You have plenty of creative drive, so be encouraged to go it alone.

Saturday the 14th. Engaging in a big day out will be high on your agenda, whether a fun time is had or not. Now isn't geared for you to be an island. Quality over quantity will count when it comes to the company you keep. Certain hearts can be tempted into risky games regarding sex and love. Adventurous spirits are set to play outside the comfort zones.

Sunday the 15th. There is always tomorrow for those of you who procrastinate. It's likely that a long-outstanding chore is given yet another rain check. Happy distractions will allure you far more than duty. The pleasure principle can dominate now. But so can the lazy principle if you're too unmotivated to move off the couch. No heavy lifting!

Weekly Summary

Bonuses and healthy tips might be offered for good performance in executing a job. You will benefit by a can-do approach and an optimistic view. Yet be wary of taking a situation for granted and treating it superficially. Do not twist words in an effort to get your way.

Subtle changes grace the cosmos. Mercury in Aries resonates with Venus in communicative Gemini. You will have more pleasure in doing business. This period can be excellent for talking things out and communicating ideas. Plans, meetings, and paperwork regarding financial support should get results. The future is augured well for commencing any type of internship or apprenticeship, particularly in public relations and investments.

A phase in better understanding physical well-being and dealing with illness might be on the way. Comprehending the mind–body connection to health is possible. A lifestyle shift could be required.

16th Week/April 16–22

Monday the 16th. The windup of a process requested by a large institution appears close. Procedures can accelerate markedly when professional individuals are invited on board. Older folk, or those possessing the wisdom of experience, are able to offer the benefit of their support. Respect received will be tantamount to the amount of respect given. A seemingly small fish is really a big one.

Tuesday the 17th. Most new jobs and fresh tasks should be off to a solid start under today's New Moon, with the promise of remarkable outcomes to follow. Tempting carrots dangled are likely to stir the ambitious Scorpio. You may take a new kid on the block under your wing, beginning a memorable relationship. Keeping the training wheels on for now, rather than getting cocky over your burgeoning ability, would be prudent.

Wednesday the 18th. Passionate switches may be turned on quickly when someone attractive approaches you. Spontaneous sexual magnetism can flare up but possibly at an inappropriate time and in an unexpected place. A conservative atmosphere and formal strictures may have to be negotiated. Anything radical or bending the rules should be curtailed. Heed the voice of authority.

Thursday the 19th. Bringing your own extra resources into a work team can transform the way a task is handled. You may possess a hidden talent that will blossom fully when you are given something to accomplish. This could lead to an increase in earnings and personal kudos. A colleague may present an investment idea, but changes to a system need to be considered.

Friday the 20th. So much to do and so little time might be the maxim today. Life can fire on many fronts right now. A variety of experiences will pack the hours. Becoming stretched in all directions will mean a certain amount of clever juggling and prioritizing. A partner in crime could come along for the ride. But his or her agenda could cause distraction.

Saturday the 21st. An offer for extra work or secondary employment may arise. It might just be a one-time job and possibly not too demanding. Caring for a pet may be a duty, or you might be working with animals. Someone you meet while walking the dog could be the next big thing. A place of learning deserves a visit.

Sunday the 22nd. Leisure time now is good for any kind of sport or physical recreation. Today looks ideal for enlisting good company to burn energy in fun and games. Jumping into an amusing pastime with children benefits the young at heart. Even getting others involved to conquer a chore seems more like play than toil. Someone's psychic impressions can count.

Weekly Summary

Strong resolve may galvanize your will to accomplish under the New Moon birthed this week. Clear your slate for a fresh attempt at an important undertaking. New doors can't open if previous ones haven't been entirely closed. Rethinking budgetary plans, workplace deals, and job descriptions appears likely. Someone in authority may be starting to change a long-held opinion. Give it time.

Most significantly for Scorpio, on Friday the Sun enters Taurus, your opposite and partnership sign. This throws the spotlight on all notable one-on-one relationships. These relationships may be personal or professional with a loving friend or a competitive foe. You will become more conscious of how you operate with others. A battle of the sexes might loom.

The heavens generally support compromise and improving the flow of exchange with other people. This is a fortuitous time to hook up with any type of specialist or guidance counselor. Someone could have a contact or information, allowing you to jump up the social ladder.

17th Week/April 23–29

Monday the 23rd. Asking the powers that be for a favor or an approval may be fraught with misunderstanding. So if you are planning to negotiate anything crucial, it's probably best to be extra cautious. Rescheduling until later could be wise, especially if an arrangement is about to become set in stone. Inadequate work and hidden catches are possible with a repair person.

Tuesday the 24th. Scorpio poise can be tested. Keeping it pleasant will be the key to maintaining harmony. Even though there is the temptation to tell it like it is, people don't seem to be in the mood for any confrontation. Pursuing a path of least resistance and rolling with any punches will be the best tactics. Most Scorpios should pass charm and etiquette school with honors.

Wednesday the 25th. This may be a day when the fairies have left some type of lucky gain lying around for you to stumble upon. You may find money in a forgotten place, or a much wanted item just serendipitously appears. Possession might be the law in an incident of finders-keepers. Getting really physical in an enjoyable way attracts another's attention.

Thursday the 26th. Precise and incisive research can reap astonishing benefits. Scorpio is the sign of the detective par excellence, always potentially able to see more than is apparent to most. Now is an excellent time to gain deep information and build on more profound knowledge. A hush-hush exchange goes well. A lover may rock your world with an exciting ride beyond your imaginings.

Friday the 27th. A pleasing person, likely younger, can appear on the scene and be perceived as a rival. Yet at the same time they're truly charming and a potential friend. Dropping any envious tendencies is advised, as you will only be shooting yourself in the foot. A worthwhile alliance might be sabotaged by intolerance. A separation could seem like a shock.

Saturday the 28th. Splendid isolation and remaining exclusive have their glamour. However, Scorpio lone wolves are likely to feel as if you are really missing out on something. Hype and spin could be circulating among loved ones and friends, stirring a restless atmosphere. Joining the boisterous antics of others will lead to unusual outcomes.

Sunday the 29th. Scorpios who took a joyride on yesterday's astrology might feel a bit jaded, but it was likely worth it. Some of you might want to continue the fun. Others will pay heed to a hankering for retreat and reflection. Spend the day quietly, whether in recovery or just lazing around. Be soothed by intimate company if you can't remain alone.

Weekly Summary

Unanticipated events can rattle you this week. Whether positive or negative, there seems to be some kind of surprise in store. Affections shift quickly, apparently without warning. Another person's fickle and erratic ways might be tiresome, provoking thoughts of separation. Guard against a quick decision, which would throw the baby out with the bathwater.

A creative project may have suffered a rocky beginning, yet now can be launched with an impressive bang. The aims of a group or a team gather momentum. Stay involved. Like-minded people bond strongly when all realize they're really on the same page. Effective inroads can be made toward notable change.

On the weekend flirtations with the weird and bizarre are likely. A risk can be taken simply for fun. Fireworks with a loved one will add an astonishing spark to life. So may an event related to a child or infant. The chance of a pregnancy occurring can be high.

18th Week/April 30–May 6

Monday the 30th. Acting on a whim, being spontaneous, is recommended now. Circumstances can have a way of falling into place quite artlessly when you have reached the decision to surrender any need for total control. Enjoy refined arts and rarefied atmospheres as much as possible today. Seek the company of someone artistically or spiritually oriented.

Tuesday May 1st. Everyone needs a degree of private time to follow intimately personal aims, especially all of you who belong to the Scorpion's cosmic pod. Now is a suitable time to recognize your individual needs and honor them accordingly. Self-sensitivity, while vulnerable, will pay. Something dearly desired can be hunted down and found.

Wednesday the 2nd. Under today's Scorpio Full Moon it can be all about you and someone significant to you. Important relationships take center stage. As long as communication lines keep flowing, an alliance may grow more stimulating and exciting. Another's objective feedback might hit the mark exactly and receive your admiration for the frankness expressed.

Thursday the 3rd. Evasive, even downright sneaky, stuff could be taking place around the home. A person in the household might be hiding something, which may undermine trust in their character. Discussion over a real estate or rental situation should be monitored judiciously. Otherwise, distortions of the facts will surely lead to a bad decision. Ask many questions.

Friday the 4th. Believing in your own worth and having confidence in a special ability could lead to making better money. But only by stepping up to the plate can any talent become duly noted. A partner or dear buddy requires some positive acknowledgment. Wearing a heart on the sleeve a little bit more than usual should be an encouragement. Be warm to your beloved.

Saturday the 5th. How to spend your leisure time may seem like a dilemma. There are many and diverse choices for having an enjoyable day. Invitations are full of color and sparkle. A spontaneous fiesta could develop when you are out with a beloved among friends. Much energy will focus on pleasure. Kids look exuberant and ready for an exploration activity.

Sunday the 6th. A neighborhood issue may be settled once and for all. Perhaps the law has been brought into the picture. All concerned with a problem seem prepared to accept some type of executive decision from authority. A nasty expense in the form of a fine might stop any protests. Even though serious business confronts you, don't get too intense.

Weekly Summary

Generally you will flow easily into the week. Some Scorpios might even be floating on the ceiling, uplifted by a sense of good grace. Compassion and empathy can be palpable presence, rendering someone, somewhere, a soft touch. Both giving and receiving are filled with benefit all around.

The Scorpio Full Moon midweek calls attention to notable relationships and the choices made with them. The intensity of emotional sensitivities can increase overall. Someone who counts makes a statement that really hits home. Themes around communication and understanding may grow. If you are not feeling heard, then what are you not really hearing?

Magnetic vibes are sure to see the likelihood of some compelling attractions. Singles may find someone noticing and coming on to you. Interesting dates with unusual partners are foreseen. Gambles with the heart are likely. If love is a lottery, take a ticket.

19th Week/May 7–13

Monday the 7th. Getting to know a neighbor may hold the potential of a greater bonding. Might even be that you know the same people, and a small-world syndrome kicks in. All kinds of social interactions can go well. However, it's wise to remain discerning with certain folk. Lies and distortions are afoot, from little white ones to alarming whoppers.

Tuesday the 8th. A loved one might announce an intention to travel or possibly will make a departure now. Today some Scorpios will be visiting a relative, probably a sister or aunt. Time is sure to fly by, as the saying goes, for those of you having fun. Amusements and quirky happenings are capable of stirring good spirits. A physical or practical joke is the order of the day.

Wednesday the 9th. Intrepid and ambitious Scorpios might be staring down the barrel of an important test. It appears a superior or an organization wants to check if you can make the grade. Fortune will favor those of you who maintain integrity and sincerity rather than those thinking that being likeable is the benchmark. Fathers and father figures appear crucial in the picture. Someone could become a grandparent.

Thursday the 10th. Greedy tendencies could prove disruptive, as rebellion erupts when someone is not getting their way. It might be especially so if your kids have wants that are stretching the regular budget. A redefining of values may need to be enforced about the nature of worth. An unexpected bill could turn out to be on the high side. A diplomatic colleague is able to smooth out a difference.

Friday the 11th. Thoughts may turn to affairs regarding shared investments or monies. Negotiations concerning loans and debts likely get underway. Credit application might turn into a tricky process, with a lot happening beyond your control. Knowledge will constitute power when you understand the details of a legal situation. Becoming informed is vital. A karmic event may touch a love affair.

Saturday the 12th. Possessive ways and manipulative tactics appear sure to get someone's back up. Bites are more likely to be worse than barks when any conflict arises. So if you are spoiling for a skirmish, be prepared. Someone might be lurking in the wings, waiting for the right cue, to fight back. Too much force and inappropriate anger are a toxic combination.

Sunday the 13th. Volatile stuff is indicated. Brooding resentments still under wraps might suddenly be purged.
Serious strain stretches a relationship to absolute taut-
ness. Everyone is prone to issuing ultimatums, and many
a bluff will be called. Fight or flight is the likely choice at
times. Little ones are best supervised. Something appears harmless but may hurt.

Weekly Summary

Significant planetary alignments speak of huge positive
potential or of crashing and burning. Basically, there
will be the brave and the foolish, or sometimes a mix of
both. Hopes and expectations rise higher in anticipating
change. This week shows a sense of expansion and pleasure in attaining new worldviews. Reflect on purpose
and meaning. Realizations and awakenings are possible.
Be open.

Steady Scorpios might find confidence beginning to
wobble if what is pertinent is ignored. Limitations and
strictures begin to tighten, as individuals or organizations close ranks. An inner toughness will show itself
when the tolerance level plummets, be it yours or another's.

Intensity mounts when Mars and Pluto, Scorpio's two
ruling planets, are in challenging aspect to each other.
But this doesn't have to be doom and gloom at all. Of
all signs, yours is one that gets remarkable results for
courage. Beautiful gems are birthed from powerful
pressure. Stay strong!

20th Week/May 14–20

Monday the 14th. A good relationship with a boss or
manager appears of value. Who you know can be a resource from which to draw support for a personal ambi-

tion. Effective moves toward producing real results appear sure to take place. Strong foundations may be laid for building a more solid future. A family member's fantasy of an apparently weird outcome just might come off.

Tuesday the 15th. Most Scorpios will rally well today against any type of adversity. A normally placid colleague could get uncommonly fired up, displaying a surprisingly assertive attitude. You may also find yourself becoming a little more strident than usual if the right buttons are pressed. Responding rather than reacting will be paramount. A degree of diplomacy is wise and constructive, too.

Wednesday the 16th. A demand to stop dreaming and start actually doing should begin to sink in. Early days with an endeavor warrant baby steps and a soft touch. A productive partnership could begin to come together on a practical level. Letting bygones be bygones might occur with another, allowing circumstances to be approached completely afresh. All sorts of beginnings are well-timed now.

Thursday the 17th. Signing up for a shared financial venture or possibly some kind of debt could be nigh. However, it's recommended you check the paperwork and contracts thoroughly. Taking the time to get clear and have any deal thoroughly assessed is sure to save potential regret. The health and well-being of a friend might bear watching, perhaps because of mental stress.

Friday the 18th. Lucky fortune streaks through the ethers, offering a brief window of opportunity. So some of you are set to strike just when the iron is hot, without even being aware of the timing. Beating others to the punch may happen without much thought, bringing unexpected delight. Be watchful for envy and resentment either within you or in a friend.

Saturday the 19th. A social event with an exotic or international touch can spice up the day. Foreign cultures and romance are likely to tie together nicely. The attraction factor is likely to increase when a person from overseas appears on the horizon. Intellectual pursuits, and intellectuals themselves, could also appeal. Shared beliefs and sympathetic ideas may well see a heart won.

Sunday the 20th. Open minds get the most out of the day. Trying the untried is exhilarating, leading to new styles and ways. A fun-filled ambience is sure to follow from connecting with talkative buddies. There may be someone a bit on the too-intense side. Hopefully, it's not you bringing the party down. Sometimes light and superficial are most appropriate.

Weekly Summary

Take advantage of energy to burn, and the pace may accelerate. Scorpio's coruler Mars zooms into fiery Aries on Tuesday. On Wednesday a New Moon occurs in Taurus, Scorpio's partnership sign. The time is ideal for many kinds of beginnings, especially if courage and assertion are factors. Jump starts and kickoffs are foreseen. Physically oriented projects, helped along by companions, are especially well supported by this week's astrology.

New starts always constitute endings. A process related to a coming finality can also begin. More decisive action can be taken toward a closure or even a total cleanup and recycling. Plans concerning surgery or any major personal changes are likely to become more tangible.

Wily planet Mercury promises stimulating, even startling moments. Interesting and unique curiosities can be discovered. Shy and coy tactics in a flirtation might not work as well as a candid romantic attack. Many ships are set to pass in the night.

21st Week/May 21–27

Monday the 21st. Passing by the middlemen and going straight to the top is an opportunity to be taken. Making a connection with those really pulling the strings will pay off rather than getting mired in red tape with underlings. Forwarding a message to an authority figure seems vital to success. Return calls and put the right paperwork in place. Be proactive.

Tuesday the 22nd. Good financial stars are present for Scorpio. It appears there is money to spend, and a pleasing item can be picked up. Past discipline and planning are likely to manifest the desired results. Meeting your goals should come easily if you have honored time-management rules. A promotion or increase in responsibility is signified. If an elder offers a lottery ticket, take it.

Wednesday the 23rd. Keeping your own counsel regarding an investment is recommended. Even the most experienced professional might make a mistake when offering normally trusted guidance. Someone perceived as holding the power could actually be a fraud. Imagination and idealism are positively enhanced. However, not all is as it seems, no matter the image presented.

Thursday the 24th. Fortune and benefit are around but have a way of being disguised. Sometimes what is really a lucky break doesn't seem like it on the surface. Such a scenario can happen to you right now. A disappointment or a loss may occur for a higher purpose, which will grow clearer as time rolls on. Respect what you have instead of brooding over what you don't have.

Friday the 25th. Prevention being better than a cure is a maxim that now fits many circumstances. Switch into survival or damage-control mode when you realize that something is unsafe. The rumblings of an impending ultimatum could be felt, galvanizing the urge to fight or flee. Not panicking, and knowing there is a solution to every problem, will reassure you. An unexpected bonus may be given.

Saturday the 26th. A distinctive token or heirloom might be passed on. Or perhaps this special something is found when you are rooting through antiques and secondhand objects. The likelihood of a possession returning, or the lost being located, is foreseen. Mindfulness doing a routine task is required in order to prevent potential mishaps. Accidents now could leave scars.

Sunday the 27th. A lazy, evasive path might be taken by some Scorpios, as time out is needed on this leisure day. Exclusive forms of recreation will cost you but are likely deemed worth it. One-upmanship over who has the best toy might degenerate into resentment. Games of intellectual superiority also can end in trouble or regret. Use focus and intensity constructively.

Weekly Summary

This week opens with the Sun moving into the sign of Gemini, the eighth sector of the Scorpio horoscope and the sector that signifies mystery, power, control, regeneration. You might be excavating secrets, coming to grips with what has been unknown. Great therapeutic and transformational possibilities are indicated. Potent professional relationships can be formed.

Pathways toward achievement and furthering career aims may now come under consideration. More specialized education could be necessary. This would hone your chances for landing a plum position. Discussions with teachers and with those in the know will be vital to self-improvement plans. A compassionate personal sponsor may be ready to lend aid by introducing a network of contacts and leads.

Beliefs around value and attraction become of note. Scorpio who is invested in the idea that looks are everything might have a beauty myth blown apart. A partner's eccentric ideas about sex can change your attitude in this regard.

22nd Week/May 28–June 3

Monday the 28th. Last-minute information makes a difference, carrying quite an effect. A decision you thought was settled may turn in another direction, according to variables only just perceived. Be prepared for change and stay flexible in order to keep proceedings steady. Words from a partner's lips can help crack a mystery. An ending might give rise to a long journey or foreign contact.

Tuesday the 29th. Creative self-expression is an excellent way of establishing confidence and personal presence. Join an imaginative group in which art and fantasy are staple ideas. Discovery of a fresh recreational pursuit could have fateful consequences around a love affair. Momentous passions could begin to bubble, and desire can grow. Use your heightened intuition.

Wednesday the 30th. Good luck if you're hankering for clarity from someone about the actual truth. Bamboozling vibes are in the air, as are contradictions that just don't match up. The benefit of the doubt might have to be employed when completely dissimilar opinions result in a confused standstill. Read between the lines. A qualified and wise person can inject some compromise into the picture.

Thursday the 31st. Attending a public event with favorite company might be the ticket to a weird and wonderful time. The presence of bohemian types and radical thinkers will make things interesting. Doing something unusual with kids will be packed with surprises. Internet relationships and cyber dates may progress. An overlooked bill will take a chunk from your wallet.

Friday June 1st. A fortunate occurrence connected with the home could distract you from the usual obligations. Still, you will have time later to address these duties. Scorpios in charge are quite approachable and openhearted today. You might even be sentimental. Parents are sure to take pride in a child's landmark achievement.

Saturday the 2nd. Security and resources may dominate your attention, and the health of your bank account may require some care. Consider making an appointment with a financial professional. This would give you an objective assessment of your money picture. Aspects of the law or a legal proceeding might feature now. Some Scorpios are drawn to make a crucial decision about the value of an item.

Sunday the 3rd. Touching base with a friend could coincide with a unique situation in which you contact more people. Impromptu fun is indicated when a suggestion flies in from out of the blue. A diverse group can make a happy band of partygoers, probably meeting in an unusual place. Whatever goes down, have a good sense of humor.

Weekly Summary

The week opens with Mercury moving into the Scorpio-friendly sign of Cancer. Late Thursday night sees a Full Moon forming to peak in visionary Sagittarius. Lofty stuff is signified. You can objectively grasp a broader picture in many circumstances. Thinking big, and feeling big, will enhance your optimism. What is happening mentally can be in sync with your emotional truth. This kind of balance can serve your well-being and quality of life very well.

Intuition is a factor that is growing and is sure to prove valuable. Hunches concerning money, whether incoming or outgoing, should be respected. Buying and selling may get uncanny results, as you know instinctively what something is really worth. Perhaps an expert inspires the right telepathic flash.

Social and communicative vibes pick up pace toward the week's closing. Comings and goings around the local area will see you with much to do. It's time to get spontaneous and gamble on spur-of-the-moment contacts.

23rd Week/June 4–10

Monday the 4th. Taking the initiative on the job will yield more than a decent return. You should be able to leapfrog ahead today, provided you have the courage of your convictions. Getting on, and doing it your way, should net you an extra bonus. Confidently slaying the competition can best be achieved with a comrade in arms. A pay dispute sees everyone jumping on a soapbox. News from afar comes in.

Tuesday the 5th. A partner might have to make a public appearance where image is paramount. Glamour and beauty are possibly related, or maybe the arts. Accordingly, you might be roped into seeing and being seen. And it's likely you will be sweetening up the right people with your magnetic Scorpio charm. A benefactor is nearby. Be open to the occasion.

Wednesday the 6th. Adjustment and restructuring could be demanded in your home environment. A landlord or condo board might pull rank, enforcing what seems to be a heartless decision. More balance between give-and-take can be regained if a certain agenda is completely surrendered. Familiar folk are ready to offer loyal support. Bend rather than break.

Thursday the 7th. You are able to show your smarts right now. The heavens bless students, writers, and all activities based on words and information. If there is an individually creative product to push, the timing is suitable for doing just that. Networking into an international arena may move smoothly. Making a wager on reliable intelligence has unanticipated repercussions.

Friday the 8th. This could be one of those days when the unexpected can be expected. In other words, a monkey wrench may be thrown into certain works. Better not choose to rush or be superficial. Reliability of others is unsure. However, there is likely much stimulation and it shouldn't be boring. Slow and steady is a pace to strive for, but stay pliable.

Saturday the 9th. Interesting and changeable vibes continue to resonate. You could simply itch to do something, anything even! Scorpio eccentrics might feel more eccentric than usual. So it's likely never been a better time to express your uniqueness. A lover could display symptoms of restlessness and may be feeling hemmed in. Remember all the sayings about loving and letting go.

Sunday the 10th. Today you have the motivation to improve something, especially yourself. You may choose to take action and change unhelpful aspects of your everyday lifestyle. But there might be some questions about maintaining focus and following through in the long term. A workout buddy, a team, or even a personal trainer can be the key to commitment.

Weekly Summary

Energy will be poured into work and home life alike. Your coruling planet Mars aligns superbly with benefic planet Jupiter. Big steps can be taken toward gain and gratification. But beware of getting too cocky and believing the wrong publicity. Nonetheless, profitable payoffs are there for Scorpios prepared to take a degree of risk and to push the envelope. Just restrain too much forcefulness and arrogance.

Love affairs and partnerships may begin to show cracks. If so, such fault lines are an indication that circumstances have grown too staid or too rigid. On-again off-again dynamics can make for a roller-coaster experience. Strive for balance.

Change is as good as a rest, it is said, but it becomes a demanding principle at times. New romantic and social interests might also develop now. The speed of interactions is set to accelerate, although fickle invitations will ruffle some feathers. A tempting speculation could hover enticingly. The higher the hazard, the greater the loss but also the greater the win. It's your call!

24th Week/June 11–17

Monday the 11th. Movers and shakers will be blessed now. Take effective action on a practical level. If the going is on the tough side, you can bet that the tough will get going. A masculine figure can help you reach some desired goals. Possibly it's someone in uniform or someone holding a degree of overt authority. Today is all about industriousness. Get cracking!

Tuesday the 12th. Affections can be displayed in a weird way. A loved one may wear their heart on their sleeve today, but their behavior still raises questions. Exciting as it might be, certain parades could be rained on by grumpy partners. Introducing someone special to the family should be postponed for now. Competitive tendencies lurk within seemingly harmonious relations.

Wednesday the 13th. Sacrifice can be constructive and is sure to leave a deep impression. Charitable Scorpio will give more than a fair share when moved by compassion and caring. Fighting for the underdog should come naturally to you. Let your higher inspirations drive your actions, and you will get excellent results. Idealism will blend well with gumption.

Thursday the 14th. The whirling dervishes among you could have spun into dizziness after a frenzy of doing. If your energy feels as if it's scattered all over the place, slow down, prioritize, and regroup. Slip-ups and breakages can be definite signs of trying to juggle too much. Consult a trusted and experienced individual who has a system, which will help you balance your duties.

Friday the 15th. You could end up in a situation in which the sound of silence seems deafening. But finding a place of repose and privacy is truly food for the soul. Stilling the mind, and the mouth, will reap much benefit. Withdrawing to study a complex and important subject is an instinct to follow. A phase of expansive research is indicated, wonderful for students and teachers alike.

Saturday the 16th. A familiar friend, currently afar, appears likely to touch base. There is delight in reestablishing a connection to a foreign or highly educated person. The words of a loved one are capable of leaving a lasting resonance. Conversations concerning religion and spirituality are featured now. There is great pleasure to be found in reading and writing. A masterpiece can be born.

Sunday the 17th. Sharp elbows and short fuses are not a good combination, even at the best of times. Toes and egos are apt to be stepped on today. A cranky encounter may flare up. Cuts and bruises await any Scorpio who displays a forceful attitude. Mindfulness is key if you are using machinery or anything related to heat and metal. Cool it!

Weekly Summary

Planet Mars is always vital to the Scorpio story. Your astrological coruler is very active now, fortuitously aligning with the Sun, Saturn, Neptune, and the New Moon that forms late Thursday night. Heaps of potential is signified for anything usually viewed as daunting. Courage and foresight are an uplifting blend to be found within yourself or within many nearby inspirational sources. Remain receptive to subtle signs.

There are plenty of chances to come clean, to be candid, and to assert your desires. Be bold and speak up. There is opportunity for healing and for turning negative scenarios into positive situations. This is possible on many levels, from the material to the spiritual. Health issues, mental and physical, can be effectively faced. Various techniques, from surgery to alternative therapies, can go well. A mysterious illness or allergy may be cured.

On Friday evening Mercury goes retrograde, deepening your sensitivities. You might retrace the history of certain beliefs and biases. Understanding your emotional investment here can lead to great learning and growth.

25th Week/June 18–24

Monday the 18th. Personal resources and special knowledge can be taken as a reflection of status. People can be easily impressed by what is assumed to be noble and right. Some people want what others have or what they value. Goodness has its own rewards now, which are apt to present themselves. Good fortune in business will promote happy moments in Scorpio households.

Tuesday the 19th. A high-impact time is indicated when you could have a big effect on happenings or be markedly affected by happenings. Focus on your mission, then go forth. Once real decisions are made and actions begin, confirmation and support will emerge. Whether you're an independent entrepreneur or are working for a company, decent earnings are in the cards.

Wednesday the 20th. Good things may come to those of you who have been waiting. Clubs and groups are featured now. A recent acquaintanceship can develop into a loyal friendship. Uncanny déjà vu may have you already knowing just what someone is going to say. Careless spending in the past might catch up with you now, as a big bill arrives. Complacency will create problems.

Thursday the 21st. Sensitivity and sensuality are heightened now. Liaisons of the dangerous style could form more readily. A fascinating attraction may compel some Scorpios to wade into a situation where you might get a little hurt. There is no room for superficiality in most interactions today. Even a seemingly casual encounter may contain a hidden agenda.

Friday the 22nd. A collection of challenges may arise now and might create a rocky path to your goals. Agile diplomacy will help you, so that you finally see the light at the end of the tunnel. Respect will be the key tactic to employ. A gutsy performance will expose true character. A hero or heroine might be born. But try not to attempt the impossible, striving against all odds.

Saturday the 23rd. If inappropriate morals and ethics are projected onto a love affair, a serious discussion is warranted. Establishing good back-and-forth communication will help to turn a negative view around and clear up a misunderstanding. Be nurturing and empathic. Realize the real emotional agenda behind anyone's behavior. Listen to a child's words and really hear them.

Sunday the 24th. Staying under the radar, out of the spotlight, is likely to be a strong instinct. But everyone could be attending an event centered on a highly revered individual. Whatever the happening, you probably will be coaxed to go. A noteworthy encounter occurs when you venture into unfamiliar social territory. You might meet a new romantic partner!

Weekly Summary

Strong dynamics color the Scorpio solar horoscope with intensity and drive this week. Major goals can be accomplished, as your willpower is galvanized and your resolve is stiffened. Your planetary rulers, Mars and Pluto, line up well together. So the iron is hot and it's definitely time to strike! Passions are likely to ignite, carrying a potent emotional charge. It will be essential to channel this energy fruitfully.

A lazy streak also resonates, perhaps promoting a path of least resistance. Pleasurable temptations and moments of ease can soften the sharp edges of ambition and striving. On the other hand, your desire for nice stuff can motivate you to work harder and earn more so that you can afford it.

On Thursday the Sun enters the sign of Cancer, highlighting your horoscope sector of travel, study, and learning. On Sunday Mars enters Taurus, your sector of partnerships. Then Sunday night the Moon enters your sign. Your charisma is enhanced, and people are attracted to you.

26th Week/June 25–July 1

Monday the 25th. Planets Saturn and Neptune in opposition today can create a pull between your intimate life and your public life. It could be time to differentiate between reality and illusion if you are deciding to take a certain direction. Unequal situations will demand rebalancing. It will benefit you to reassess previous discussions and data already gathered. An educated person has a good tip.

Tuesday the 26th. Extreme mood swings may sweep over the sensitive Scorpio. You might experience both anxiety and anticipation about a coming change. A loved one can be acting in a risky manner, making for thrills but also insecurities. Twists and turns, plus ups and downs, will inject variety and stimulation into this mixed-up day. However, emotional intensity can create a physical drain.

Wednesday the 27th. Choose carefully the lens through which you view the world. Seizing the day with a refreshed attitude will be a helpful approach. Perceiving a glass as half full rather than half empty isn't as unrealistic as it can seem. Positive beliefs will attract pleasing results, as long as your self-confidence isn't just a concept in your head but really felt in your body.

Thursday the 28th. The chance to take a spontaneous vacation might arise. This could have connections to young folk or to exploring a different culture. A return to a location recently visited could be on your agenda. Travel for educational purposes or to attend a spiritual workshop is possible. Study will awaken your curiosity. An advanced degree could be your ticket to big money.

Friday the 29th. Closing down a financial account or an investment deal will likely be swift and straight to the point. With many choices of actions before you right now, there may be no going back. One door may be shut forever, clearly marking a phase in development. Before you set off on a journey, make sure the household is safe and secure. Homemakers will be busy cleaning and organizing.

Saturday the 30th. Musically minded Scorpios, as well as those of you who take pleasure in anything gorgeous, will be in your element. You could be attending an excellent performance where imagination creates an otherworldly time. The Full Moon can also create a romantic day. Seeing a movie in loving company might fulfill your entertainment wish. Writers are able to create magic based on historical facts.

Sunday July 1st. Often a lull occurs after a Full Moon, and that's the tone today. Routine correspondence, errands, and the daily commute can seem a letdown in the wake of emotional anticipation. Don't mistake ordinary for boring. Now the road to success is the obvious one, familiar and regularly traveled. Loyally attending to duties will be noticed in high places.

Weekly Summary

Saturn tinges all affairs this week, forcing the emotionally vulnerable and sensitive Scorpio to toughen up in order to handle worldly affairs. Stay with the bird in the hand rather than hope for a dream come true or divine intervention. You could feel a little isolated or out on a lonely limb. Use this period as a test of your togetherness and ability to manage external demands and pressures.

Perhaps parental expectations are proving stressful and unrealistic. Or maybe it's the boss who is being too hard with impossible standards and deadlines. Attempt to do your best on your own terms, and tell others to back off so you can get on with the job. Genuine communication, person to person, will be a key in resolving differences. If that fails, there is always the law or higher authorities.

Put in the hard yards, and there should be rewards aplenty. But they come from persevering with unpleasant or disagreeable tasks. There are no prizes for flying off with the fairies in the hope of fantasyland outcomes. Success in business and love comes through commitment.

27th Week/July 2–8

Monday the 2nd. Staying at home today might cause trouble with someone. Maybe your partner has an axe to grind and you're their target. An impatient customer or client could be on the warpath because you're absent and not giving them the attention they want. Self-discipline may be sorely needed to prevent overreacting to outbursts or attacks. Defend yourself, but don't overdo it.

Tuesday the 3rd. An official showdown or legal situation requires more thought. Cultivating private dreams is essential to balance the burdens of everyday existence. Rather than complain about a job or decide to quit, look for an engaging event or situation outside work. Pursuing romance means calling on the courage of your convictions, not just wearing your heart on your sleeve.

Wednesday the 4th. A playful mood lightens the atmosphere and raises spirits on this Fourth of July holiday. The company of kids and fun-loving adults is a tonic to being overly serious. Singles can make promising contacts if celebrating the day with festivities. Risks and long shots may pay off today, just don't count on it. Whatever else is on your plate, enjoy a pleasurable date with your partner.

Thursday the 5th. Fun is in store for the young at heart and Scorpios with a sense of humor. If agendas are rigid or intolerant, a yearning for unusual detours and amusing distractions may cause tension. Travel and vacations are uppermost for many of you, especially parents with younger children. Be open to left-field suggestions and serendipitous possibilities. It's okay to change the plan, again.

Friday the 6th. There is pressure to handle from the get-go this morning, which is likely economic. Let this motivate your efforts because only action will ultimately make a difference. Still, doing the wrong thing would be worse than doing nothing at all. Pause before charging ahead, or else you could retrace your steps and do it all over again. Travel plans may be on hold because of work demands.

Saturday the 7th. Difficulties in travel can arise, likely causing frustration. It might be better if a partner or companion took the lead, although they may be unable to help you. Moneymaking ventures can easily run afoul of legal requirements, causing altercations with official-dom. You might feel as if you are held for ransom by threatening lawyers. Make sure you have one on your side.

Sunday the 8th. A busy, productive morning comes easily for the fit and motivated. Do chores you have been putting off and get them out of the way. Then devote time to one person whose company is compelling or arousing. Whether it's sexual attraction or the need for a sparring partner, a magnetic charge builds. Empathic conversation leads to physical closeness.

Weekly Summary

As inconvenient or routine as it may be, attending to home duties comes first as the week starts. Refinements and adjustments to domestic life can proceed in the face of heavy workloads and relationship frictions. Take comfort in the refuge you have created for yourself. It's from this base that you can renew the will to handle life's challenges.

The best way to lighten up and revive dampened spirits is by breaking out and having a fun time, at least for a day or two midweek. Kids are always a source of youthful energy and joy, and their playful enthusiasm can rub off. Making new acquaintances, with a sensual agenda in mind, comes more easily than you might anticipate.

A retrograde Mercury in Cancer, your travel sector, continues to deter plans for smooth travel. Perhaps it's better to stay put. Then you can enjoy experiences on the love and career fronts. Much can be accomplished. Roll up your sleeves, get your hands dirty, and continue to learn through doing.

28th Week/July 9–15

Monday the 9th. A feisty sexuality permeates the mood early on, and physical expression comes naturally. Whether it's duty or desire, your instinct prevails. Daily schedules may leave little time for lingering with a loved one. This may prove a major frustration, but blaming anyone else misses the point. Later, attention turns to worldly affairs. Tonight Mercury comes out of retrograde mode and goes direct.

Tuesday the 10th. Pleasing a partner or lover could prove difficult. Be receptive to their needs, even though they may have trouble expressing them. Reading between the lines is important to avoid unnecessary conflict. Keeping customers or clients happy might also be a problem. An overly fussy person seems to find fault with even the most attentive efforts. You will win some and lose some today.

Wednesday the 11th. A renewed burst of enthusiasm may grip those around you, as the prospect of real progress reemerges. Let thought precede action for the moment. You need to reorient yourself as to the expectations of others. Among all the crazy ideas and short-lived, shortsighted schemes, there are sure to be a few pearls and gems. Understand what is truly healthy for you and follow that path.

Thursday the 12th. A clash of wills and purposes marks a potentially stormy encounter. If both sides insist their cause is righteous, there is no meeting place. Authorities should be heeded now and allowed to call the shots. It may be a parent or a boss, but if you respect them, listen up. Stick to a current plan while fresh possibilities take shape. The world is a big place with many options.

Friday the 13th. This may not be your lucky day, but it's not an unlucky one either. Cultural events and social entertainment can broaden your perspective. Scorpios with a sense of humor find much to enjoy in diverse encounters. Beginning a course of study may be part of the excitement. Embarking on an overdue or postponed journey will come as a relief for travelers.

Saturday the 14th. A New Moon in Cancer suits Scorpios very well. The urge to strike out into the wider world and make a unique mark propels you out of the house and onto the road. Waiting patiently for slower companions can only frustrate scouts and pioneers. Tell them you'll get back to them later. Gambling or risking in the global marketplace offers a possible breakthrough.

Sunday the 15th. What you know and who you know serve you well today. Business opportunities are in the ethers for Scorpios prepared to strut their stuff. A chance to put your learning on display appears to be a highly rewarding experience. With the courage of your convictions, you're at your persuasive best. People will warm to your ideas.

Weekly Summary

To start this week, Mercury picks up speed and moves forward again. You have probably learned something in the last few days and weeks that is really worth knowing. Sometimes it takes a while for understanding to arrive. But when it does, everything looks different. Movement, communication, learning, and information transactions can all make steady progress. If you have been waiting to go somewhere, now is the time to get on your horse. If you have been wanting to study something, now is the time to sign up.

The agendas of intimates and colleagues are sure to influence you. Yet try to steer clear of anyone else's rigid ideas or obsessions because they will likely slow you down. The pace of life increases midweek, with many Scorpios becoming exuberant about bigger life potentials and roads as yet untraveled.

Once Venus enters Virgo on Saturday night, social life beckons with gracious companions and charming encounters. Mind your manners. Try not to take offense, even when it's bluntly intended.

29th Week/July 16–22

Monday the 16th. The chance to make a dream a reality arrives today if you can see it. Hiding behind a mask of stem duty or disciplined routine lies the face of extraordinary achievement and success. But, like all great art, it takes ninety-five percent perspiration to make it happen. Believe in yourself and others will too. At least one solid supporter stands behind you, whatever happens.

Tuesday the 17th. Memories of past loves and bygone friendships can be pleasant and reassuring, reminding you of your former life. More than one person in your circle is likely to remind you of past characters you have known. Enjoy good company where there is sure to be flattery, and possibly seduction, in play. Watch for a charming salesperson who wants to sign you up.

Wednesday the 18th. A hunger for physical and mental excitement might take you by surprise as you behave in ways somewhat out of the ordinary. A reliably placid partner may also be seeking unusual stimulus, lending support to adventurous proposals. New acquaintances quickly become firm friends. You have much to learn and gain from people met now. Don't let old hurts hold you back.

Thursday the 19th. Meetings and groups are best attended first thing. If you're in charge of scheduling any gathering, make it a morning event. Getting together with people for whatever reason is likely to become a gabfest, making it hard to stick with agendas. A quiet evening suits, despite what others may propose. In-depth investigation of a favored subject relaxes.

Friday the 20th. News of another's good fortune may not be what you want to hear. It's possible to like and love people despite what they think or do. Try to distinguish between the mind and the heart. Politics, religion, and the big issues require deep consideration and a personally meaningful spin. Take a healing break from worldly cares in a quiet refuge or sacred space.

Saturday the 21st. Despite a gut feeling you're missing out on what is happening, you're better off staying in and keeping under the radar. Meditation and undisturbed breathing space will reward with a clarity of vision and a sense of inner purpose. Artists should pay attention to their concepts or inspirations. Dreams offer wise guidance and light the path, even when the way becomes dark.

Sunday the 22nd. With the Moon entering your sign, you emerge from hidden lairs to enjoy the day on your own terms. Expressing yourself comes easily. Lively conversations take up time and attention as you reach out to connect with people and the world at large. The urge to visit a sweetheart can motivate a short trip. Smart, sharp characters are entertaining.

Weekly Summary

Career and professional interests are front and center. Doing your duty, or at least your levelheaded best, is essential to retain your place on the ladder of ambition. But it isn't long before an urge for fun and pleasure bubbles up and social life regains momentum. A brief spell of partying takes the stage.

By midweek, burning the candle at both ends no longer suits, and it's time to take stock of where you're really at. Allow yourself the grace of some downtime, and stand back as your partner takes over daily affairs.

The possibility of an exciting love affair, from a distance, could preoccupy you. Or you will be consumed by spiritual practice and artistic expression.

Parents considering the educational future of youngsters may begin to steer them appropriately or respond to their enthusiasms. A learning opportunity or a long-distance lover may grab your attention. Whatever seems hidden, unknown, or mysterious might be revealed by week's end.

30th Week/July 23–29

Monday the 23rd. A strange standoff could develop between you and an antagonist who openly opposes you. On one level it's clear what the issue or difference is all about. Yet other factors may lie beneath the surface. These can cloud judgment and dampen the possibility of reaching agreement or understanding. Stubborn defiance won't work. Be compassionate, put yourself in their shoes.

Tuesday the 24th. It would be easy to become disappointed and even discouraged now. Attempts at progress and reaching ambitious goals may be blocked, misunderstood, or discounted. Draw energy and attention back to yourself and start there. Your self-esteem is likely to be tested temporarily. Taking your sense of worth from others, professionally or socially, is neither appropriate nor healthy.

Wednesday the 25th. Spirits are up again today. Your sense of humor and perspective returns. In contrast to a recent sense of isolation, there may now be too many people to cope with. Being in a crowd reminds you of what you share with many others. It's also a great opportunity to make a buck. Don't look a gift horse in the mouth or shy away from getting what you need from others.

Thursday the 26th. Strong purpose is at your disposal. Make good use of it in the right directions. A major purchase can be a consuming, exhaustive process, but the result is sure to be worth the effort. A partner may not understand or appreciate your financial plans and decisions. Nevertheless, stick to your guns, as you're likely to be proved right. Cash flow and net worth will tell the story.

Friday the 27th. Skip glamorous events and highly touted public performances. The best theater is right at home or on the job. Stick to the ordinary, grounded daily grind for best results. Conversations in the office should entertain and take the edge off drudgery. Short trips and errands with a purpose may need action. When out and about, remember to look your best.

Saturday the 28th. There's a low-key buzz in the neighborhood, making it worthwhile to get out on the street. Flea markets and store sales may offer one or two genuine bargains for careful shoppers. A community event involving the kids may require your presence. You are likely to weigh spontaneous recreational suggestions against other duties. A bit of both is likely.

Sunday the 29th. Arrange a gathering or party for this evening at your place. The Full Moon is a perfect backdrop for any celebration. Whatever the occasion, people are in the mood to come together. Family affairs can reach a climax and most probably in a positive way. There may be a housewarming or the announcement of a new arrival.

Weekly Summary

When the Sun enters Leo on Monday, it's career and performance time for Scorpios. Put your best foot forward, make your mark, and be seen as effective and present in your worldly duties. Yet this might be easier said than done because a thorny aspect between Mars and Neptune can cloud affairs with uncertainty, misunderstanding, or possibly deception. Taking action and following through could be tough, especially if critical or essential things are left up to others.

Venus going retrograde on Friday won't help to make matters any easier or clearer. At best, there will be the development of a wonderful friendship and good feelings within a group. At worst, it may be an invitation to fiddle while things begin to fizzle.

Sharp thinking and an understanding emerging from the history of recent events should assist you in making necessary decisions, discriminations, and judgments. Intuition should steer you well, but it demands applying a degree of wisdom and timing.

31st Week/July 30–August 5

Monday the 30th. Shopping for household needs may be your immediate priority. If you're not in the mood to face the world, send someone else or order home delivery. Feeling out of sorts is distinctly possible, both emotionally and physically. Treat the symptoms, then delve into the underlying causes to resolve problems. A chance to heal means taking the tough medicine that is required.

Tuesday the 31st. Do the tough stuff first. Then it's likely to be all downhill, letting you take it easy and loosen up. Unpleasant situations are best left alone for now. Other tasks may also belong in the too-hard basket, at least for a time. Meanwhile pleasure calls, and the only decision is whether to pursue it alone or with company. Involvement with boisterous characters looks to be part of the deal.

Wednesday August 1st. You can never have too much fun, even when times are tough. A detour from the well-beaten path would be a tonic for your spirit. Taking a chance on life and love seems risky, but you'll never really know unless you try it. A spirited lover will turn the tables on negative emotions, perhaps taking you by surprise. Loosen up and step lively!

Thursday the 2nd. It will be embarrassing, or worse, if you lose your emotional cool when you should keep it together. This applies especially on the job or when you're in the public eye. Parents can find it a stretch to juggle touchy kids and a needed career. Enlist your partner's support or pay for necessary help. Foolish financial gambles can go awry.

Friday the 3rd. Getting that desired job or a promotion seems in the cards if you're in the running. Motivation from a partner or colleague can only go so far in keeping you on the ball. Dig deeper to find your own reasons for applying yourself. Money and prestige are there for Scorpios who make the effort. Responding to customer feedback and supplying a real demand will pay dividends.

Saturday the 4th. Work today if you must because it's another powerhouse period for making headway and getting things done. Lovers may feel neglected or disagreeable as a consequence, but those are the breaks. Make it up to them later by bringing home the bacon, along with an elegant gift expressing your loving devotion. Then hook up with amusing pals for a night out.

Sunday the 5th. Relationships are on the firing line, and dissatisfactions are likely to be expressed. Pay attention to any situation that seems unhealthy or unwholesome. If it's not doing you any good, then it's probably not doing anyone else any good either. Parents or in-laws who are feeling poorly can put stress on everyone. Support them, but don't let them lean on you.

Weekly Summary

Rocks and hard places might see Scorpios experiencing a tough week. Seemingly relentless pressure is on both career and relationships. Maybe it's the boss or your partner who is having problems. But if they are being squeezed, then inevitably you will be in the line of fire or caught up in the drama. Take challenges seriously, yet use discretion in any response.

The atmosphere is set to lighten midweek, as the Sun and Jupiter are in sync. A celebration may be timely. Look for a grand opportunity in business. Expect a reward for successful performance. Jump on board any ride that is going in the right direction. And that direction is toward enhanced earnings and greater prestige.

You can climb to the top of the ladder in your field or profession, with the responsibilities and advantages of such a position. Just be careful that any advance is not to the detriment of family or private life. Health could also suffer through overlong working hours and unrealistic expectations.

32nd Week/August 6–12

Monday the 6th. Parental disapproval of a personal relationship can be emotionally distressing. You may be required to stand shoulder to shoulder with a compatriot who is under heavy stress. Courage and fortitude could be needed to withstand a formidable obstacle. The situation is likely more complex than it appears on the surface, but you will ultimately know where you stand.

Tuesday the 7th. Hidden or obscure matters might explode into the open today, with intimate secrets or confidential information exposed to the world. Scorpios who have been scrupulously honest in your dealings will have nothing to fear. But somebody has probably been hiding something, and it can totally unravel now. Take care in financial dealings, and beware entangling alliances.

Wednesday the 8th. If yesterday you didn't entirely believe that honesty is the best policy, you might be more convinced today. Your integrity and loyalty will be rewarded by those who depend on such attributes, especially where money is involved. Refinancing property or borrowing to provide for long-term family needs may seem a daunting prospect. Yet it can be arranged effectively.

Thursday the 9th. Recent resolutions and determinations should leave you feeling more relaxed. The open road calls, and journeys can be enjoyable and smooth. Group learning is helpful in grasping large concepts and gaining overall perspective. Personal self-expression has a ready-made audience, larger than imagined. Artists, promoters, teachers, and performers have the green light. Go!

Friday the 10th. Legal formalities need attention for Scorpio seriously contemplating marriage or another committed partnership. Widely explore all possibilities before going forward. A freewheeling mood makes an early weekend a seductive possibility if you can get away. Travelers and foreign countries spice up the mix, with lively contact in person or on the Internet.

Saturday the 11th. A lineup of planets in regal Leo could be too excessive for Scorpio tastes, grating on your sensitivities. Prima donnas are likely to prove tiresome in their self-obsessed need for attention. Nevertheless, you might as well stand back and enjoy the fireworks. Business and career are in a stellar phase in which the only way seems up. Use good publicity to further your aims.

Sunday the 12th. Events and affairs become deeply fused and intricately interrelated. The focus of today's New Moon in the sign of Leo may be a formal celebration or a gathering. Families constellate around elders in a period honoring births, marriages, and deaths. Enhanced prestige, bestowed honors, celebrity, or fame may come to the deserving.

Weekly Summary

Of major note this week is the strong, positive connection of Saturn and Pluto, which are in fire signs. A depth of commitment, joined to unstoppable courage and boundless enthusiasm, can be the gift of the times. But you may have to dig deep to uncover such treasure. Remember, all that glitters is not gold. Perceiving the essence of things beneath the surface is important. In practical terms it sets up the possibility of achieving much that you have been working toward.

With Jupiter poised to move ahead in your finance sector, the economic future should start to look even brighter. A large purchase may have been occupying your mind, and you will want to decide whether or not to go ahead with it.

Venus retrograde slides into Leo and Mars enters Gemini. Sexual politics and gender differences emerge for discussion and understanding, or at least make an appearance on the agenda.

33rd Week/August 13–19

Monday the 13th. A romantic love story can have a happy ending for someone you know, maybe even yourself. But ultimatums and critical decisions in affairs of the heart should probably wait a little longer before you sign on the dotted line. Professional and commercial ventures can reach a plateau. Greater progress here will need further development.

Tuesday the 14th. A friend's enthusiasm can be infectious to the point of disrupting routines. This may become a wild ride, but there is sure to be stimulation and learning. A group program or publicity campaign could commence with much fanfare and develop into a fair share of chaos and opening-night jitters. Enjoy the company of notables.

Wednesday the 15th. Competing demands on your limited resources can make you tense and touchy. Needy friends might want to borrow cash or expect you to pay the bill when out together. Even if you can afford it, their presumptions likely annoy you. Choose the company of prosperous, generous souls who don't need you or your money. Hopefully they will just enjoy who you really are.

Thursday the 16th. There may be no chance for rest even if you feel you could do with time out. If you get an opportunity to back off the stage, take it. If need be, shut the door of your office to work alone without being disturbed. It might be that you will have to take important work home for further research and preparation. Quiet family time suits you this evening.

Friday the 17th. Dreams offer instructive guidance for worldly affairs. Keep a notebook handy to jot down details upon waking. This is your deeper self speaking to you, so listen up. Dramatic flair and beautiful romantic touches will impress your lover. Don't hold back. Going over the top will be appreciated even more. It may not be your style, but make the effort anyway.

Saturday the 18th. Don't rush to get up this morning. Sleeping in for extra rest will do you good, no matter what else the day holds in store. Later, once the Moon is in your sign, you will feel like making an appearance. A formal social event is right up your alley. Dress to impress but with a twist of unique style that grabs attention. Formidable contacts are there to be made.

Sunday the 19th. This day is meant for taking it easy. No doubt there is a heavy load on your plate. But it can wait until tomorrow, while you have fun today. Sports, games, and multimedia entertainment all hold appeal, ideally to be shared with loved ones. Scorpio pleasure seekers are in your element. Where you go, others are likely to follow. Set the pace.

Weekly Summary

The luxury to dream and take it easy might be curtailed by absolute necessities on the career front. You may feel like one character when in private or at home and another in public or on the job. Parents could concern you now, as their hopes intertwine significantly with your affairs. Make no mistake, though. The focus now is on your working life, vocational advancement, and the resulting financial growth and security.

Performances of all kinds are featured strongly. It might be very easy to burn out, so pace yourself for the longer haul. Any small window for a break should be grabbed with both hands. The enterprise should be able to do without you for a day or two.

Major celebratory events with grand themes and even grander settings are likely in this period. While you may not be the center of attention, or pleased with certain decisions or results, take part in good spirit. Let go of any resentments, allowing others to have their hour of glory.

34th Week/August 20–26

Monday the 20th. You're not the flavor of the month today, so don't try pushing your luck too far. Receive criticisms with respect and dignity, even if they are emotionally punishing, and learn something. Parents and bosses seem to be down on you. Yet infantile or impotent reactions and defenses won't get you far. Live to fight another day, and take it on the chin for now.

Tuesday the 21st. Being lazy won't do you justice at present. Others are expecting a lot of you, and they will be sorely disappointed if you let them down. Schedules seem too flexible, making it hard to coordinate effectively with people. Spending an unduly long time on unimportant matters and not enough on real business would be a mistake.

Wednesday the 22nd. Reaping economic rewards for hard work should raise your spirit and improve your mood. You will be glad to see the Sun leave Leo and enter Virgo. But what has been hard can make for solid success. The urge to shop could be hard to resist. Be generous if you can afford it. Ensure that major purchases are stylish, close to your heart, and of good value.

Thursday the 23rd. Make a bright start at all costs. Otherwise you might miss out on the main event. A commercial proposal now holds high promise of profit and success. Don't be surprised to find greater responsibility and authority heaped on your shoulders. Just make sure you're being well paid to take on extra burdens. Communications and meetings will prove effective.

Friday the 24th. Conversations while doing the rounds can be loaded with gossip about who is in charge or who is going to be in charge. Information you receive today is likely accurate but sharply barbed and with certain agendas firmly in place. So read between the lines to determine where you stand with your peers. Remember, though, you are not in a popularity contest.

Saturday the 25th. There is nothing to be gained by going over and over a project, task, or problem. Forget making yourself look good by pretending to be on the job. No one cares anyway. Instead, focus on matters of direct personal importance. Study is favored if you apply yourself. A solitary walk in a park or through a garden can be instructive.

Sunday the 26th. Enjoy a lively day with your partner and family. There's action aplenty around the old homestead, and it looks to be of the wholesome variety. Relationships with men are set to improve. This can touch everything from finances and business to your physical well-being and sex life. Bringing warring parties together at your place provides a forum for negotiation.

Weekly Summary

It is a serious and weighty start to the week. The pressure is on in the workplace. Living up to expectations and putting on a good show will be really important. This can be a make-or-break time for many Scorpios. So forget lazing around and taking it easy, or be prepared for the consequences.

The Sun moving into Virgo on Wednesday will come as a blessed relief for Scorpios. Who you know and what you know become equally important and are likely connected. Old contacts may prove invaluable in opening the right doors. Club memberships could be expensive but are sure to be worth the price.

Chasing big ideas and biting off more than you can chew would be unwise. Promising options may be dangled in front of you, but only one will be right for you. A cranky, disagreeable partner should be susceptible to sweetening up. Put your romantic foot forward, but also hear what they want. Take active, positive steps to heal conflict and resolve differences.

35th Week/August 27–September 2

Monday the 27th. You will want to focus on your hopes and ideals for the future in contrast to the actual facts of everyday reality. You will never accomplish or experience what you can't imagine, so get dreaming. You can probably afford a taste of luxury now, so go ahead. Just be clear that you are taking a temporary time out. Fantasy will be soothing. Books, movies, and music appeal.

Tuesday the 28th. Greedy gamblers could get creamed today, especially Scorpios inclined to take tips from other bettors. Parents will struggle with the inevitable expenses of raising kids. Don't let them pull the wool over your eyes about the cost of things. A new love affair might unfold for singles at this Full Moon. But the accompanying lunar eclipse at dawn warns of possible pitfalls, especially with money.

Wednesday the 29th. A small lapse into recklessness may prove unfortunate. Playing fast and loose with hard-earned cash would leave regrets and a bitter taste. The same applies even more so to fooling with people's hearts or affections. It might be a case of do unto others, so bear that in mind if temptation arises. Protect your own vulnerable sensitivity, as waters run deep now.

Thursday the 30th. Out of the blue, you may be asked to take someone's place or perform extra duties on the job. That will keep you very busy, but the pay should also make it worth your while. A partner's inconsistent behavior with money may mean you need to earn more to fill the gap. Don't worry, though, what goes around surely comes around.

Friday the 31st. If you love what you do, put in a full day of effective and motivated effort. Avoid any temptation to cut corners or go home early. Pushing on with a project, right up to the last minute, will be rewarded with satisfaction and success. Overtime may seem unappealing, but it could make all the difference in accomplishing an important goal.

Saturday September 1st. The time is ripe for dating and socializing. So grab favorite company, even if it's your own, and get out in the mix. Entertaining distractions are just what the doctor ordered. Kicking back and forgetting hassles will refresh your soul. New friends, maybe even new lovers, seem to be available for those of you looking. Get going!

Sunday the 2nd. An old friend's dependability is like gold. Powerful information can be packaged in a short sentence. What seems to be an insignificant statement can produce major repercussions, triggering a cascade of reactions for positive or for negative. Perturbing as it feels, this is a suitable time for entering intimate territory in a deep and meaningful relationship.

Weekly Summary

Peer groups, like-minded allies, and networks of associates are what the Pisces Full Moon on Tuesday draws attention to. Love affairs and parent–child relationships are also spotlighted. A total lunar eclipse accompanies this Full Moon. So there can be quite an amount of questioning, and all kinds of alliances come up for grabs. Thoughts and talk of change will impact on various associations.

Working hard and playing hard might light a few Scorpio candles at both ends. Hopeful hearts can anticipate special happenings, with fun and camaraderie. Organizing a unique celebration in the workplace probably demands much of you, but enjoyably so. People you thought were staid will show their silly side.

Major news on Sunday is Saturn's shift into Virgo, a sign supportive of yours. The ringed planet of keeping it real to get real results now gets to work restructuring greater plans and wishes. Some deconstruction may be needed in order to build a better future. Time and time management will be allies, as long as you commit to concrete goals. Walk the talk!

36th Week/September 3–9

Monday the 3rd. Unanticipated events, plus the erratic tendencies of other people, may combine to cause a change of plans. Organizing a group for recreational purposes likely will require more effort than you supposed. Unrealistic expectations may go unfulfilled, leading to disappointment. It appears that there will be more satisfaction in one-on-one interactions than in crowd dynamics.

Tuesday the 4th. Healing and transformational processes are set for an injection of energy. Many improvements may leap ahead. You will spot light at the end of the tunnel. In most cases physical activity and stimulating exercise hold the keys to betterment. A partner may be unprepared to change an opinion about what is of value. Don't beat your head against a brick wall in frustration.

Wednesday the 5th. Energy is best invested in contacting an organization or an important associate earlier rather than later. Availability and easy negotiation might be compromised if you wait too long. News of an upcoming significant retirement can start circulating, although gossip is best discounted. A quiet meeting with an older person may get others whispering. Don't buy into hearsay.

Thursday the 6th. Sparky vibes can put a spring in your step. A positive attitude naturally attracts positive results. So embrace that principle. Scorpios who are truly lucky and in an upbeat zone will have the advantage. Good fortune seems mostly a matter of being in the right place at the right time. Another point to remember is to assume nothing and expect anything. Chance is quirky now.

Friday the 7th. Extra work taken on behind the scenes can keep you taking care of various odds and ends. When you are left to solo devices, your efficiency should increase, with nothing being overlooked. Particular responsibility for a boss's information might fall into your hands. Much communication and connecting could unfold privately and in an exclusive place. Find a solitary retreat for study and writing.

Saturday the 8th. Pleasantries, grace, and saving face are today's redeeming factors. Smooth operators are capable of disarming you with a charming smile. Scorpios in the business of beauty and pleasure might be onstage somehow. Go with the flow, be diplomatic, and leave ego at the door in order to maintain good relations.

Sunday the 9th. Weak links in an affair could show, making for uncertain feelings. Changes in relating, if ignored until now, are sure to be needed. Some kind of separation seems to be in the offing, causing maximum stress. Be aware of changes of heart and capricious desires. Romantic passion might infuse a platonic friendship. Rebels easily find their causes today.

Weekly Summary

Scorpios can glide into this period under the auspices of a good Mars and Venus alignment, plus the added bounce of an exuberant Sun and Jupiter combination. Life should be full of spice, or at least some piquant moments. Exciting corners may be turned, likely in the most unplanned ways.

Bittersweet touches are also signified. An unexpected ending brings on a curious mixture of perturbation and happy relief. Someone might be moving to a place where access is curtailed. Just touching base on a casual basis is no longer to be taken for granted. It could feel as if a hole is being left by an absence, which will never be refilled. But there can also be opportunity.

A friendship or romance may feel like a magic carpet ride. Yet magic carpets don't have safety belts and can take crazy directions. Letting go of control, surrendering to an experience, is a tempting test. At the weekend your defenses will soften. Scorpio hearts might open to risk and whimsy.

37th Week/September 10–16

Monday the 10th. Joining a particular group or organization might burden you with expensive fees. Becoming accepted is likely dependent on a process that is out of your hands. The worth of an enterprise could be overhyped and needs to be brought back into realistic proportion. Borrowing and lending are prone to hitches. Giving an inch right now will mean someone takes a mile.

Tuesday the 11th. A fresh face can enter, introducing an unusual element. Differences, unnoticed before, can now be under consideration. You could realize that someone is using their resources to manipulate you. The seeds of a separation or ending may be sown now. On the other hand, a whole new personal network can be nurtured. Embrace change, whether it is material, intellectual, or emotional.

Wednesday the 12th. Quietly mull things over and reflect on recent events. You are compelled to seek privacy, away from all distractions. You might even stay completely under the covers, preferring to sleep on something to come to terms with it. Opting out and being buried away will make you noticeable by your absence.

Thursday the 13th. Great opportunity can be presented through subtle and small means. Scorpios who are attuned to the radar will be in line for special insights, lending the kind of information that gives you an advantage in many situations. Amiable and receptive vibes are all around. So make the most of what they have. Only optimists should apply today!

Friday the 14th. With the Moon entering your sign of Scorpio today, you can get on the case and pursue your desires efficiently. By applying a bit of judicious discretion, an incisive strike can be engineered. What was thwarted a few days ago should be achieved effectively if you follow up now. Support will come once you take the initiative and assert your independence.

Saturday the 15th. Scorpio lonely hearts might see the flirtation bus pulling up for boarding. Make sure such potential isn't sabotaged by moping around in splendid isolation. An encounter appears as if it were destined to be. Sexual magnetism can feel palpable when a certain someone sends the right signals. A pretty trinket for a special person might attract a lot of attention.

Sunday the 16th. Aspects of glamour and fantasy can entrance you. There is delight in entering another world, or at least dreaming about it. Rose-colored romantic hopes might mask the reality that an exceptional affair is only fleeting and that there might be some disillusionment ahead. A potential intimate partner is best viewed as an acquaintance.

Weekly Summary

Scorpio is connected to recycling and rebirth principles and is extremely resourceful. You can access assets both outside of and within yourself, leading to marked change. You may decide to develop your innate talent, honing your ability to a high aptitude. Treats and pleasures might be cut back to achieve larger goals.

Tuesday's New Moon and solar eclipse in Virgo will stimulate your horoscope sector of future things to come. Any sensations of restriction and boredom could feel more pronounced. Dissatisfaction with not following your heart can catalyze major reform and change. Radical adjustments in direction might occur. Stronger links could be forged with those already on another path, which you also truly want to follow.

Many things begun now might experience wobbly first attempts despite all your passion and drive. A strong emotional investment makes for vulnerability, so take early steps mindfully. Friday's Scorpio Moon strengthens your confidence and faith in yourself, great for dipping a toe in various waters.

38th Week/September 17–23

Monday the 17th. Making something happen effectively could be fraught with sticking points and hassles. A con-

servative institution wants everyone to play by the
rules. But both aggressive and defensive tendencies
arise and must be monitored. Conflict resolution by an
objectively reasonable voice might be necessary. All
bets are off in fierce legal battles.

Tuesday the 18th. Charity beginning at home is a maxim
that comes into play. A family or household member
may require support and goodwill. Be prepared to drop
the criticisms, the judgments, and the finger-pointing.
Graciousness and compassionate regard should hold
sway and be appreciated. New information will be illu-
minating.

Wednesday the 19th. An associate's secret doings and
business games could be put on the table for all to view.
Someone in a group probably feels quite betrayed and
may let it be known destructively. Remaining a team
player is sure to become uncomfortable when any dis-
honesty is detected. Healthy skepticism is wise when a
deal, to good to be true, is put forth.

Thursday the 20th. There is a good chance that you can
make up for any perceived deficiencies in your behavior
toward a loved one. Subjects could be rehashed, with
positive outcomes all around. A past tiff probably had
deeper effects than was apparent back then. Encourage
candid disclosure. Be empathic, especially with kids.

Friday the 21st. Unsettled resentments may bubble
away more toxically than usual. If something is going to
give, it probably will do so today. High tension might
ready your reflexes for fight or flight. Survival modes
are likely triggered by what is or is not communicated.
Do not believe all that you are told. And do not imagine
the worst if you are told nothing.

Saturday the 22nd. Taking up an invitation to visit and stay at a friend's place will be beneficial for all involved. Conversely, another person could be enjoying your hospitality. Short trips and pleasure jaunts, without any social pressures, will be good therapy for Scorpio. Some happy wandering around the neighborhood can lead to places of delight and discovery.

Sunday the 23rd. Change is in the air. Today the Sun begins its monthlong transit of the sign of Libra. Libra is the sector of your horoscope that signifies the psyche and psychic wisdom, the area where the unconscious meets imagination. Places of retreat and worship might beckon, stirring your spiritual side. Or the pleasure principle may be enhanced. Seek artistic, aesthetic, and poetic surroundings.

Weekly Summary

This can be an empowering time for Scorpio individuals. Changes in your lifestyle are your focus, and assertiveness is your approach. But willfulness and power plays may result in a standoff. This is a signal to let something go. As a second wind blows, like the phoenix you will rise again. Many challenges can be met and conquered.

Relationships between parents and children, brothers and sisters, and other relatives are highlighted. Family assets may come into play. You can ultimately benefit from a piece of land or other property. Start investigating with the idea of developing it into an independently run business.

You may want to terminate a shaky friendship. Before acting ruthlessly, think it over. Talks to improve a relationship will be successful if you do not come on too strong with the criticism. Gentle astrological influences offer love, inspiration, and respite. Enjoy various pleasures but not to the point of escaping your responsibilities. Don't lose focus on the real picture. Buried and unseen are the seeds of transformation that are now germinating.

39th Week/September 24–30

Monday the 24th. An associate's dispiriting opinion will make you seek further feedback. Any disparaging remarks by only one person shouldn't be allowed to discourage you so easily. Even a respected authority could be out of touch with current norms. A quick-thinking friend can solve a problem by offering last-minute guidance, making all the difference.

Tuesday the 25th. Expenses for loved ones can mount up when you are hunting for perfect gifts. You may be shopping for yourself but make a spontaneous purchase for another. An item spied may bring a dear one to mind, which will encourage sentimental spending. Scorpio parents might have children who insist on pricey toys. Teach thrift, discourage waste.

Wednesday the 26th. This day of a Full Moon is packed with punch, motivating quite a few gutsy performances. Taking quick action may be what it's all about, but not rashly or with too much force. Unthinking and mindless reactions will lead to mistakes, even a costly incident. Consulting a specialist would bring a situation into objective focus. Listen well to an impartial analysis.

Thursday the 27th. Generous and amiable moods create a receptive environment. Take advantage of people's good graces and hospitality. You can find just the right words to steer a satisfying outcome your way. It will not be hard to display a nice attitude and courteous manners. A pleasant demeanor attracts assistance, favors, and tips.

Friday the 28th. Your opinions and knowledge might be desired by others, inviting you to pass on some inside information. Scorpio teachers, speakers, and writers can feel strong creative fires in the mind. A lecture tour or publishing deal will mark acknowledgment of your intellectual work. Aficionados of foreign cultures may make plans to travel and see the world.

Saturday the 29th. An old friend may be spending more time with a new friend. Your buddy may even be having romantic feelings and want to start a love affair. Loyalties and jealousies all tangling up are likely to create confusion. Issues about separation can stem from your disgruntled feelings. Insensitive behavior may also arise when distractions make you neglect a loved one.

Sunday the 30th. Prejudice displayed at a social gathering can turn you off someone. An associate might show an unappealing side of their nature, putting bumps in smooth relating. Too much reliance on one person's integrity can create certain consequences. Some Scorpios may decide to join the military. You will excel in basic training.

Weekly Summary

Not all races are won by the swift, not all prizes go to the strong. Use brainpower and smarts. The Aries Full Moon is excellent for thinking sharp and actually following through. Coordination and physical reflexes are enhanced, suiting creative activities like dancing. Mental games may be skillfully played.

It gets better! Both Mars and Mercury move into receptive water signs, your coruler Mars into Cancer, and Mercury into your sign of Scorpio. Maintain independence of thought and beliefs. Cultivate sensitivity to subtle emotional messages. Read between the lines. A phase of great education and of personal wisdom is augured. Travel and international affairs become important themes.

This week is good for initiating negotiations, also sorting or signing paperwork. Networking and advertising will benefit from thinking outside the box and exploring fresh avenues. It's okay to be bold and to be heard. It's also vital to listen, really listen.

40th Week/October 1–7

Monday October 1st. Scorpios walking any financial tightrope without a safety net might feel a decided lack of balance now. If you are stretching a budget to the max, living hand to mouth, this may start to take a toll. Unexpected and costly emergencies could convince you to turn negative spending habits around. A parent or mentor gives you a pep talk.

Tuesday the 2nd. Healthy debates take place when a valued belief system is under challenge. Religion, politics, and cherished sacred cows can motivate impassioned stances in defense of a viewpoint. Much learning is possible in any kind of dynamic exchanges. Virtually every experience will be a tutorial of sorts, teaching you heaps. Others, too, can learn from you.

Wednesday the 3rd. People at the top could smile on you, perhaps with something special to transfer as a favor. An individual thought difficult to deal with may disarm you by displaying a friendly receptivity. Once a problem is approached openly, it's likely to be no problem at all. Formulating and exchanging unusual ideas with an old associate will pass many hours pleasantly.

Thursday the 4th. Getting a bigger picture comes from grasping a situation's unseen flip side. Fancy detective work might be needed when particular facts just don't match up. Some Scorpios might even employ a professional investigator for the job. Bosses and superiors are apt to be insulated within their own personal kingdoms and on unrelated flight paths.

Friday the 5th. Communication should flow well as long as you listen attentively. Anyone liking the sound of their own voice too much might be called to task for discounting another's words. Misplaced confidence and pride can serve to undo a lot of previous hard work. A beneficial reward can come if you keep a friend's confidence. Show loyalty.

Saturday the 6th. Focusing your passion with laserlike effectiveness is a natural Scorpio talent, which may be well used now. You could get on the case ferociously when something, or someone, becomes the object of intense desire. It seems the more beautiful and exclusive anything is, the more compelled you will likely be to acquire it. Power and money talk big when splashed around.

Sunday the 7th. Serious talk may unfold regarding education and training. A person well-qualified in their own right is worthy of mentoring you. Generally, mature and experienced folk can help you get practical. Plotting out future paths and wider possibilities will give you increased encouragement. Any target has to be clearly identified to score a bull's-eye.

Weekly Summary

Expressions of affection and desire are apt to intensify. So will your ambition to make your mark and be respected.

If the love of anything or anyone is true, there can be profound payoffs. People who count will notice when your heart is in it and will respond positively to your integrity. A rise in status is quite possible. Or there could be greater recognition and validation of your talents.

A gift may be received, which can advance your career prospects and help in doing a job with finesse. There is also the opportunity for a pleased superior to offer you a better position. You might be socializing with the big guns, the people who make or break a situation. Business and pleasure could mix intimately at times. Temptations send out a siren call and steal attention. However, remain wary and heed your survival instinct.

Relationships commencing now are sure to contain a passionate magic. The fascination factor can increase all week, stirring deeper depths than you ever realized.

41st Week/October 8–14

Monday the 8th. The workweek starts on an auspicious note, with lovely planet Venus entering the Scorpio-friendly sign of Virgo. The Moon and Saturn are also in Virgo, so you should be doubly committed to pull with teammates in order to accomplish an important mission. Extending yourself will have tangible benefits such as improving your skills and earning more money.

Tuesday the 9th. Today poses the likelihood of bumpy rides and rocky moments. A clash of beliefs might lead to radical actions. Restlessness and rashness color the atmosphere, making for unreasonable reactions at times. The grass will seem greener everywhere but home. A freedom-loving partner may feel hemmed in and want to embark on a path of independence.

Wednesday the 10th. Fast and judicious moves behind the scenes can wrap up a process. An ally has the needed contacts and may pull just the right strings on your behalf. Big projects related to big organizations may sweep you up. New plans on the drawing board hold much promise for success. If an associate is treated impolitely, the seeds of undoing are sown.

Thursday the 11th. Today's New Moon in Libra brings gentle empathy and peace to Scorpios. In the extreme, an urge to withdraw completely may take over if you want to recover from anything unsettling. Remain in familiar territory and seek a soothing silence. Even if you have obligations, find time to tune out the busyness. Be receptive to your intuition.

Friday the 12th. Honesty is a policy that will go a long way today. You cannot suppress the truth or champion something that goes against your code of ethics. Candid disclosure is a part of your integrity. Friends will be very supportive when you declare how you really feel. With the Moon now in Scorpio, you can enter a zone of remarkable personal effectiveness.

Saturday the 13th. Getting out of the house is a good call if you feel swamped by the confusing issues of loved ones. The more unusual a person seems, the more they will appeal to you. A foreigner may show their interest in a manner considered strange but will charm you nonetheless. A meeting of the minds can occur, leading to animated discussion and amazing discovery.

Sunday the 14th. Second thoughts about where you're at in a relationship should be heeded. Is your steady dating partner ideal for a long-lasting affair? For some Scorpios, the boundary between platonic friend and romantic companion has been breached. Or an exciting new paramour may be better suited as an acquaintance rather than a lover.

Weekly Summary

Dynamic astrology jump-starts this week. On Monday benefic planet Venus moves into Virgo, your horoscope sector of associations and aspirations, groups, and goals, and promises fortunate outcomes. Quiet Scorpio achievers who have toiled in private might finally be seeing the fruits of such labors. Feelings of liberation and change burst forth when a major project winds up.

Thursday's Libra New Moon offers a chance to re-align your strategies and to regain your equilibrium. On Friday Mercury starts moving retrograde in your sign of Scorpio, urging you to review very private territory. A period of soul-searching will be interesting. What has been said or thought can be revisited and rehashed for better comprehension.

Be wary of becoming either too picky or not picky enough. Everything in moderation and balance is the maxim now. Being obsessed with anything connected to personal intimacy puts you in a danger zone. Be kind to yourself.

42nd Week/October 15–21

Monday the 15th. There is pleasure in a group reunion, as fond regards are exchanged. People who shared a previous transformative experience will recognize the deep bonds formed. Today's appointments might be brief because you have a chance to make money instead. Spending may involve expensive choices. Little ones may act strangely, raising questions about their health.

Tuesday the 16th. Sometimes it's best to tell a youngster the truth. Kids can be strong when tough stuff happens. Talk of revisiting a country already seen with a friend might mean a trip to a travel agent. Scorpio in a long-distance relationship will touch base in whatever way is possible. A kind teacher can give you study tips that will quicken your learning.

Wednesday the 17th. Scorpios who have been sitting on something to say for a while might find that today is the day to present your ideas. Promoters, writers, and speakers can engage in a flurry of creative concepts. Networking and advertising will see good outcomes. Now can be a time to reach out and establish many connections both in the local environment and farther afield.

Thursday the 18th. Bantering with a person who is stimulating and fun will put a sparkle in your day. Pleasing encounters with neighbors are likely, as you get to know more of the local area. Be spontaneous and adaptable, without trying to control the way experiences unfold. Helping nieces or nephews with their homework can be a learning process for adult Scorpio as well.

Friday the 19th. The first half of the day is good for running errands, short trips and visits, and business meetings. You might be introduced to certain folk you never thought you would meet. Some Scorpios may become involved with a select few in secret negotiations, which will lead to gratifying results. Respectfully acknowledge a benefactor's help.

Saturday the 20th. Visiting any place where diverse people can mix will be fun this leisure day. Street fairs, farmer markets, and cultural festivals will draw an eclectic crowd. A happy medium can be reached at home between the young and the old. The trick is to have a variety of creative materials that cater to everyone's tastes.

Sunday the 21st. Now is built for education, entertainment, especially with familiar folk in the picture. Relatives could invite you to join an outing or a function in their home. Even if you are flying solo, you will want to be surrounded by stimulating people and events. Enjoyment and edification go hand in hand if you attend the theater or visit a museum.

Weekly Summary

This week's astrology reveals a favorable Venus and Mars and a retrograde Mercury in your sign of Scorpio. These astro influences are beneficial indeed for many interactions and associations, whether professional or personal. This period generally suits socializing and drawing on a greater network of people power. Anything to do with promotions and public relations has heavenly support.

Romantic sensuality and meaningful communications can create memorable loving moments. Expressing your true affections will go a long way in winning over someone hard to get. A first date can quickly develop a level of intimacy. Scorpios already in long-term relationships may also feel the cosmic spice. Committed partners will do well to remind each other of the original magnetism and charm that drew you together.

If you take the time for effective self-review, you will know what adjustments to make in how you present yourself. You will become aware of the potency of your views and how the smallest word can have a profound impact.

43rd Week/October 22–28

Monday the 22nd. Self-confidence about your resourcefulness, combined with passionate belief, can be a formidable asset. Scorpio entrepreneurs and opportunists can be in the motivated zone and on the mark. Good inroads in international dealings can be made now. Hesitating may lead to loss, so act swiftly. Friends are likely to distract you, but delightfully so.

Tuesday the 23rd. You might want to put off what should be done now. A state of full denial about something crucial could affect some Scorpios. Perhaps the instinct to wait awhile is right if you have to make amends to a lover or friend. The ice needs time to thaw out. Later today the Sun enters your sign, and everything should be perceived differently.

Wednesday the 24th. Sensitive feelings and moody reactions are apt to take hold. If you ignore this possibility and let crankiness dominate, be prepared for the consequences. Customers or colleagues may act a little short, pressing your buttons. Take a deep breath, then rise above such occurrences to diffuse your anxieties. Push hard to get what you wish for.

Thursday the 25th. Feeling very separate from others can be perceived more starkly now, compelling you to make contact. Be it a friend or lover, someone clear and logical can offer an objective stance on a relationship. Remaining obsessed over a betrayal will aid no one. Dogmatic values may need to be abandoned. Take the blinkers off. Reassess ideas about love and worth.

Friday the 26th. Significant Scorpio relationships are being illuminated by the Full Moon in Taurus. The Moon makes positive planetary contacts all day. This is ideal for keeping favorite company and amiable friendships. Special dates and social treats can be indulged. A night out for pleasure is foreseen. Late partying could see an encounter during which fast-talking business goes down.

Saturday the 27th. If you were out partying late last night, this could be one of those lost days. Foggy perceptions and perhaps some forgetfulness might be the consequences. Even if you are full of beans, energy can still be low. Easing into the hours, floating through whatever unfolds, is advised today. Escaping into music and movies at home should appeal.

Sunday the 28th. You may attend a celebration or gathering filled with interesting and talkative personalities. Diverse characters, cultures, and age groups may be brought into meeting range. Expect the unexpected. It appears that friction can arise from the differences. Agreeing to disagree would be best, as nobody seems prepared to shift ground and to compromise.

Weekly Summary

The Sun enters your sign of Scorpio on Tuesday. Happy birthday, and a happy personal new year for the next four weeks! This period is ideal for any type of reflection and self-improvement.

Matters of personal concern and individual wants are more likely to take precedence. Having some healthy self-centeredness won't go astray. Engaging in anything warming to the heart and soul should produce deep gratification. Enjoy what turns you on. But do take a good look in the mirror and brush up your act.

Everything in balance is still a prime maxim, and it's not all about your ego needs. The Full Moon draws attention to key relationships. There is much value in a loving partner or dear friend. If you are single and desire companionship, it seems that the opportunity for a romantic encounter does exist. But the major question arises: What kind of relationship are you having with yourself?

44th Week/October 29–November 4

Monday the 29th. Copping out to relax or knuckling down to productive effort will be today's quandary. Even if you are in a commanding position, the dilemma could still develop. The disciplined and responsible Scorpio will probably soldier on valiantly, realizing great progress and results. Or some of you will choose to follow more sinful delights while work is put aside until tomorrow.

Tuesday the 30th. Solid action can take place. Jobs are done thoroughly and with enthusiasm. Team projects and group endeavors are especially filled with constructive potential. An unusual creative factor is also afoot. Leading by example is crucial. People may rally together for a common cause. A family spirit creates good emotional bonds as shared beliefs are validated.

Wednesday the 31st. A learning or teaching environment could be the forum for romance. It is also good for meeting a new best friend. Some Scorpios might have a crush on a teacher or on a study buddy. Whatever the details, making connections and education somehow go hand in hand. Old gripes and gossip may pop up. Someone is at it again, bellyaching and backbiting.

Thursday November 1st. Be careful of what you wish for because you just might get it. Strive to rise to the top in some fashion. Stepping into a position of prominence may be what you want, but it can have stresses. Attainment isn't all it's cracked up to be when someone more superior makes their presence felt. Diplomacy is the better part of valor now.

Friday the 2nd. Bumpy moments with familiar folk can be smoothed over when certain values are reinforced. There might be haggles over household bills and related expenses. But a roundtable conference can improve the atmosphere if all involved are honest about who is really responsible for what. Someone could be funneling hard-earned resources in a detrimental direction.

Saturday the 3rd. Dynamics within a peer group or in some kind of regular meeting could be getting staid. A person may be using their older age and experience to pull rank on others. Traditional or set ways will have their good aspects. Yet they appear in need of discerning modification and adjustment. Weird encounters seem like karma when strangers find long-lost connections.

Sunday the 4th. This day is set for physical activity and all variety of active recreation. You can also find fun in mental games and humorous debates, all approached with an open regard. Parents will find kids full of beans and restless to do something. Serious Scorpio athletes are capable of notable achievement and personal bests. An international opportunity is foreseen.

Weekly Summary

The Sun in your sign of Scorpio is nicely aligned with Saturn and Mars this week. You may feel especially effective at asserting a position and striking forth to achieve goals. You will be cultivating career objectives and strategies to reach such aims. Enough mulling over and preparation may come together into concrete doings. Go-aheads and approvals are possible. If you are prepared to focus and put aside distractions for now, you can accomplish a lot.

In contrast, other heavenly action is weaving through the week. These will be promoting lush and indulgent vibes. So enjoyment and extravagance might become problematic. Do not be complacent, taking just any path of least resistance.

Beware of a tendency to think everything can just magically turn to gold. This would sabotage you. The real advantage now comes from sucking it up and making an effort. Taking careless gambles on any level might be fraught with challenging consequences. This is quite different from taking what is called a calculated risk. Don't get greedy!

45th Week/November 5–11

Monday the 5th. An associate can regale you with all sorts of details about a business or investment idea. A pretty and promising picture is apt to be painted about possibilities to come. Prudence is wise if you're asked to bring personal resources on board. Lending a receptive ear is one thing, but it's best to stop there. Secret and unseen elements are indicated for the unwary Scorpio.

Tuesday the 6th. Jealous wrangling over a possession or a person is apt to leave resentful emotional fallout. Someone is likely to perceive betrayal, no matter if an outcome is actually win-win. Exception may be taken to a colleague's use of flattery to manipulate a bigger slice of the pie. Legal battles can turn ferocious, especially around a divorce or final separation agreement.

Wednesday the 7th. The saying that life is a lottery is now very apt for Scorpio. Upbeat stars speak of moods lightening up, and plenty of lucky potential surrounds you. Silver linings are really in any dark clouds. Welcome the unexpected. Remain open to the spontaneous. That will get you the most out of this day. Feel free to do your own thing, your way. Be individual.

Thursday the 8th. Someone's defenses are set to soften considerably. They may be your own if you've recently been in any kind of battle mode. You can use your own sensitivities to understand those of another. Arranging a rendezvous for an equitable conference appears a useful move. An issue can be sorted out privately, probably surprising you with the final results.

Friday the 9th. Seizing the day and striking while the iron is hot would be a suitable approach today. Any creative Scorpios are sure to fire right up, with brilliant concepts and avenues of expression. A little reflection, turning attention inward, will likely lead to some eureka-style moments. Even the most cynical among you can have your interest excitingly stirred. Fortune favors the unique.

Saturday the 10th. Everyone needs time out once in a while, especially Scorpios. Flying solo could even be enforced, as others may be unavailable for socializing. But keeping to yourself and being lonely are not the same thing. If you take pleasure in your own company, you should really enjoy it now. Many personal delights can be enjoyed in solitude.

Sunday the 11th. All varieties of addiction and addictive tendencies may be a focus today. Some are positive, like pouring energy into a compelling creative or devotional pursuit. Others could be negative or undermining, such as substance abuse. A friend seems helpful in facing the facts and supporting any exercise in reconstruction. Don't be a complete island. Reach out.

Weekly Summary

A truly mixed bag of cosmic tricks appears now. This week could open with a diplomatic challenge to handle. Oversensitivity mixing with intensity can produce a toxic and volatile brew. If there are grievances to be aired, irritation might finally see them rising to the top of your agenda. Avoiding trouble when you let let off steam will be a test for some of you.

Soon enough the heavens lighten up, offering some scintillating cosmic stuff for Scorpio souls. Lady Luck may embrace the curious, plus those of you prepared to walk paths less traveled. Daring moves are possible, especially when you are having fun.

This period is pregnant with much to discover about yourself! Friday's New Moon takes place in your sign. And clever Mercury enters your sign on Sunday. Heightened self-perception is the gift of such astrology. Using subjective tendencies and thinking, really thinking, should lead to amazing insight. Now is ideal for all starts and restarts related to personal improvement.

46th Week/November 12–18

Monday the 12th. All good plans aside, budgets can be broken, credit limits stretched, and debts accrued. The culprit appears to be your eye for the alluring, which will cost you. Also enticing will be anything in your comfort zones. There is good money news, though. Some Scorpios may receive a big fat gift, possibly a windfall. A household member could be part of the action.

Tuesday the 13th. If you buy into the notion that there is a degree of fatefulness in the world, you could see this concept validated today. An encounter can take place that, on hindsight, seems like it was meant to be. A relative, possibly a sister, might decide on a career move, taking them far away. Trouble looms when a neighbor's value judgment brings in the authorities.

Wednesday the 14th. Speaking up and being heard could result in honest opinion and frank response. Polarizing arguments happen readily when they involve who is right or wrong. Academic qualifications don't necessarily equal smarts. Just give someone enough rope and you'll see. Scorpio speakers should be prepared to answer tricky questions.

Thursday the 15th. Legal and bureaucratic processes starting now are likely to go on for a while, quite possibly into next year. So might any ongoing ethical and moralistic disagreement. Differences in core beliefs might lead to factionalism and separate camps. However, most Scorpios should be able to rally and stand your ground. Just don't be too intense.

Friday the 16th. An upcoming family event may see a lot of primping and preening going on. Negotiations for a piece of property should proceed your way. Scorpio organizers and administrators will be in your element, calling the shots and delegating tasks. Compare notes with a reliable real estate agent, someone who is also a friend.

Saturday the 17th. Today is not really about pleasing yourself but about pleasing the people deemed closest. So it will be worth it to sacrifice your individual wants to connect with parents or grandparents. Being generous of heart and spirit will be more deeply appreciated than you suppose. Spending quality personal time with others in your clan should be relaxing.

Sunday the 18th. Today Scorpio could be a sounding board for friends and lovers who need to work out ideas and issues. A pal may want to hear your thoughts on a troubled relationship. It will surprise you when someone considered wiser and in control requests your input on a tricky matter. Research on an important project can take hours.

Weekly Summary

Try to be flexible through a flurry of communications and errands. Local transit might get feisty, with breakdowns and traffic jams. Frustrations leave a feeling of driving with the brakes on. Think patience, and count to ten before making rash calls.

Most notable for Scorpio is your coruler Mars going retrograde from Thursday until next year. This retrograde Mars will be in Cancer, a fellow water sign, generally signifying helpful potential. So a phase begins, ideal for reviewing and developing greater knowledge. New understandings and an improved worldview will grow, sometimes from what appears repetitive or slow going.

Your feelings may fluctuate about exactly what actions to take. This can create delay, perhaps even procrastination. Nonetheless, going backward to eventually go forward might not be as silly as it sounds. Appraising and reconsidering a major long-range vision could be the route to success.

47th Week/November 19–25

Monday the 19th. Talk regarding intimate stuff, like romance, love, and sex, doesn't faze the classic Scorpio type. Intimates as well as friends want to explore these subjects with you. Ethical and spiritual dimensions of sensuality may come under discussion. A lusty dance between lovers is set for an exciting spin. Your desire factor will get a decent workout.

Tuesday the 20th. Self-improvement intentions backed up by a burst of drive could see you starting a fitness kick. Motivated Scorpio may leap eagerly into a brand-new activity. Or you might resume a regimen you began once and abandoned. All kinds of second winds and second go-rounds are written in the stars. First attempt or not, the challenge lies in the follow-through.

Wednesday the 21st, Lights of genius may wait in your mind's wings today. Turn on the right switch so that the sparks coalesce into bright ideas. Innovation, invention, and creativity are highlighted. Dealings with youngsters and youthful people might carry an unusual twist. New concepts and views will get you going. A technical or scientific breakthrough is foreseen.

Thursday the 22nd. A new phase begins on this Thanksgiving holiday. Your attention may turn to money, income, and personal security. The realization can dawn as to what is really going on when it comes to value and worth. You may think about pursuing a different set of goals. A collaboration under consideration seems to have merit.

Friday the 23rd. Relations within the domestic sphere could end up in a tangle when all sorts of stories start flying around. Contradictory versions from different sources are apt to bewilder. A tale can end up so tall that it should be dismissed out of hand. Scorpio back at work might be negotiating pay and promotion with the boss, so show that you truly know your stuff.

Saturday the 24th. A partner or close friend may invite you to an interesting gathering. Or you may be paying a duty visit to the in-laws. Whether or not you dress to impress, do not be fooled by people who show off shiny assets and display designer labels. An image can mislead, especially under today's Full Moon. Keep your integrity intact.

Sunday the 25th. What begins as pleasant is capable of becoming more so as the hours unfold. Even if the day has an unsteady start, most scenarios should smooth out nicely. However, a taste of luxury might make you want too much of the good life. Sweet and giving moments are possible with close companions. Positive reinforcement helps to build a talent.

Weekly Summary

Beauteous Venus and intellectual Mercury are still in your sign, and assertive Mars is in sensitive Cancer. These astro influences may pose a dilemma about the choices you make. To compromise or to insist may be the question. The difference between love and lust could be another puzzle. Try not to pressure a dear one by demanding affection. Some burning desires can't always be fulfilled the way you want.

On Thursday the Sun enters Sagittarius, your horoscope sector of finances and assets supported by other people. The monthlong Sun in Sagittarius is ideal for examining how your resources and security are holding up. On Saturday the Full Moon falls in Gemini, your sector of personal finances. So cosmic attention is definitely drawn to all your money dimensions. Hopefully, your attention is drawn there too!

If you have something to say and nothing to hide, be totally candid expressing yourself. Use your heightened reflexes and wits to handle difficult challenges productively. Have confidence in your mental faculties and ability to learn.

48th Week/November 26–December 2

Monday the 26th. True moments of epiphany await seekers of spiritual knowledge. You may visit a holy place or attend a lecture on a sacred subject. A perfect message can appear, as if by magic, when you turn to just the right page in just the right book. Higher guidance is all around and taking many shapes. Scorpio devotees of yoga, dance, and other forms of artistic expression may reach exalted levels.

Tuesday the 27th. Ideas and information can be gained in a variety of ways. Using digital means to access data swiftly will open up a greater network of contacts and knowledge. The service and repair of electrical gadgets should go pleasingly. Any expert you approach right now should be willing to present credentials and references. Otherwise, be wary.

Wednesday the 28th. If you're dealing with someone in charge or even a representative, later in the day promises the warmest reception. Negotiating a satisfactory price and percentage is more likely then. Someone may bend the rules for you. A simpatico newcomer to a group may quickly become a good friend. A charismatic individual can validate and uplift your beliefs.

Thursday the 29th. Doubts and disillusionments threaten to deflate your balloons, making you question your inner strength and self-confidence. But perhaps it's just your ego that is unsounded. Putting too much reliance on what others think of you can be the problem. A supposedly trusted supporter may be vacillating in their loyalty to you. Be true to yourself.

Friday the 30th. Rebels need not apply right now, as the heavens bless anything that is honored by time and tradition. Observe the rules and regulations when you are in a formal environment. Respecting etiquette and heritage will be vital to achieving your aims. A board or a committee might require you to make an accounting on an important matter. Some Scorpios can end up in a courtroom testing the limits of the law.

Saturday December 1st. Yesterday's serious and formal tone can echo into the morning hours. A friend may have an issue with you. A past disappointment can have you feeling wary and on guard. By afternoon astro influences promise favorable conditions and experiences. Take the initiative to make amends and clear away doubts.

Sunday the 2nd. A streak of intense cosmic luxury decorates the heavens. Serendipitous delights abound. You might succumb to your favorite temptations and special treats. Overindulgence can happen when something is just too good to refuse. Have pleasure, by all means. But quality over quantity is recommended if you want to stay in balance.

Weekly Summary

Some of the most fortuitous and pleasant planetary contacts grace this period. Benefic Venus and Jupiter are wonderfully in sync. Neptune beguiles. Scorpio imaginations should be on full power. Those of you in the business of fantasy and pleasure can be rushed off your feet. Certain alliances are sure to prove very useful, especially if a favor is owed to you.

The catch is that all these flowing astro alignments may not be the best for getting down to brass tacks and getting concrete business done. Those of you wandering in a helpless fog might be challenged and tested. Limitations and restricting conditions may also be felt more tangibly now.

Certain events can put a chink or two in your ego. But any discouragement or disappointment has a greater purpose than what is immediately apparent. When personal weaknesses are exposed, there is opportunity for you to see where work on self-concepts is necessary. The good things in life may still be had as long as you stay on track. Perhaps a reward system is worth consideration.

49th Week/December 3–9

Monday the 3rd. A carefully chosen gift or service that you provide is apt to have a resounding effect. Someone will be profoundly touched by receiving your thoughtful regard. Opinionated values and dogmatic stances can be changed dramatically. As you dredge up things long forgotten, you can learn from them. The past might haunt you, yet it is a valuable resource.

Tuesday the 4th. Refined and sanguine atmospheres are easily created whether in imagination or practice. This is a time for gentle and affectionate expression. Lyrical and poetic touches are appreciated. Dropping your stubborn Scorpio resistance in order to cultivate trust and faith can be hard. But letting go does have special benefits. Remember, though, release and sacrifice are two different creatures.

Wednesday the 5th. Personal appearance can be used to a strong advantage. Scorpios who take care to present a positive image are most likely to get positive results. A smile and a kind observation won't go astray either. Dressing to impress will do just that, boosting a better sense of self-worth. You can enjoy a bit of primping and preening, whatever the variety. Do whatever feels right.

Thursday the 6th. Feedback from a loved one may be something you really want. But fishing for compliments will not satisfy. Victory is empty here if it is demanded rather than earned and given freely. Mutual admiration clubs can form spontaneously now if you just let them. Dropping your expectations and remaining open will get you true validation.

Friday the 7th. Surprises are in the works, some of which could be unwelcome. So better not put all your eggs in one basket. A serious deal you thought was already finalized might experience a disruption. Negotiations may be reopened, catching you unaware. A love affair can heat up when you least expect it. The timing of clocks needs adjustment.

Saturday the 8th. Plenty of gumption and elbow grease should be applied to an ongoing project. A lot can be accomplished. A group may invite you back for another talk because of your positive impact on those in authority. People are receptive to your ideas. Groups endorsing a cause are very effective now, possibly making headlines.

Sunday the 9th. Entertaining loved ones at home should be an interesting pastime when a notable item is displayed. The object could have something to do with another culture. Foreign languages and publications are highlighted. Under today's New Moon, a fresh financial approach to a family business may arouse spirited discussion. A parent can have a visionary idea.

Weekly Summary

The Scorpion classically symbolizes passion and privacy par excellence. Clandestine love affairs are signified. A strange liaison or a coming out might create a stir. A secret romance may begin. The strength of your affections and need for intimacy will be realized.

On Wednesday Venus enters your sign, gracing it for most of this month. Venus in Scorpio enhances your magnetic appeal plus your desire to love and be loved. Whether partnered or single, it's from all about your personal expression and connecting with others. And the Scorpio Moon from Wednesday until Saturday is a period for beautifying the self and improving social graces. Any makeover started now should reap extraordinary benefits. Lavish tastes and chocolate cravings are things to watch out for. You could compensate by feeding on sugar.

Despite possible unsteady times, you can go from strength to strength. A diamond in the rough is worth polishing. Organized action and a well-planned strategy will get positive outcomes.

50th Week/December 10–16

Monday the 10th. Scorpio shoppers could be scrambling to find fine presents for the holidays. It might be a case of the bold or the banished, as any lack of chutzpah would mean missed opportunity. Surely your eagle eye will spy a bargain. Not only massive discounts but also massive expenses will be scored. A legal or educational fee may loom large now.

Tuesday the 11th. Another crowded day is likely full of stressful busyness. If you have just begun to prepare for the seasonal celebrations, you might react in a panic. Take a deep breath and sit down. Then plan what needs to be tackled first, next, and so on. One thing at a time. And don't abandon it until it's finished.

Wednesday the 12th. Take a leaf from an associate's book. Think constructively, act steadily, plan practically. Obligations and duties will be no sweat if you approach them with a can-do attitude. Most business affairs will go well, especially when everyone is realistic. Conservative folk and formal situations are likely to be more pleasant than you anticipated.

Thursday the 13th. Good news in the mail and interesting happenings at home are foreseen. You might receive a fascinating object, a payment, or a visitor. A message or phone call could stir everyone's imagination and set tongues wagging. Use your intuition, also common sense, if a loved one is suffering in silence.

Friday the 14th. Supporting the less fortunate or mentoring an underdog will have its own rewards. Themes around compassion and charity are strong right now. The message to share and share alike is clearly heard when a dear one is in need. Arrangements to baby-sit a family member, a house, or a major possession can be made. You will be caring for someone or something special.

Saturday the 15th. Wanting to get hold of an exclusive article could escalate into an obsession. Extraordinary effort can be applied, to the point of an international search. The really determined Scorpio will have plenty of stamina to locate the desired goods and have them safely delivered. You might forgo, or even forget, a friend's party because you have bigger fish to fry.

Sunday the 16th. Fiesta and fun are in the air. So Scorpios who haven't partied yet may well do so now. Light-hearted variety will appeal to you, the more unusual the better. Keeping favorite company should be the order of the day, whether in a crowd or one-on-one. You can also have a great time enjoying solo pleasures on your own.

Weekly Summary

On Monday the Moon joins the two mighty planets Jupiter and Saturn in the sign of Sagittarius. Then on Tuesday Jupiter and Pluto are conjunct, an event that happens only every twelve years. Irresistible forces and tremendous drive are in the ethers.

The sign of Sagittarius represents your horoscope sector of money, value, and worth. So these astro contacts are excellent for strengthening your convictions, your faith, and your beliefs. Your willpower should be like steel when it comes to making a buck. But equally strong might be a desire to spend big. Watch for being overconfident and extreme.

Venus still in Scorpio makes wonderful star contacts, and the fantasy factor of Neptune is also on stage. Components of love and lust may be equally aroused, especially if you are imbibing. Wider and deeper facets of sexual intimacy can be discovered, lasting affections can develop. Even if single, and loving it, you should feel particularly good in your own skin, as beauty is obtained from within.

51st Week/December 17–23

Monday the 17th. Delays and stumbling blocks are primed to arise. Paperwork plus the ins and outs of researching details can be the culprits here. Perfection is a nice concept but not a practical one. A dogmatic stance may prevent you from achieving a gratifying deal. Trying to beat a system appears to be futile. Don't bite off more than you can chew.

Tuesday the 18th. Outrageous fortune can make an appearance, as benefic planet Jupiter enters the sign of Capricorn today. Scorpios could be lucky in cards and in love. Material and social windfalls may occur, with the right gain and with the right people. Uplifting news about a loved one will warm your heart. Caring contact with a child reinforces a very special bond. Aunts and uncles are important.

Wednesday the 19th. Intense trepidation with a crucial decision is only natural. Consider beyond the superficial because what you commit to now is likely to be a long-term deal. A very special promise might be given to or received from a partner. An important contract may be set in stone, with no backing out allowed. Draw on focus and precision in order to build something lasting.

Thursday the 20th. Relatives and extended family could be a prominent presence. Siblings seem particularly important, especially those younger than you. Someone near may call a conference of close confidantes. Together you all can plan a landmark celebration and pay heartfelt respects to a generous spirit. A network of loyal people is growing, and with it your optimism.

Friday the 21st. A fatherly figure's blessing on a partnership will bring grateful happiness. Approval from on high may come through for Scorpio applicants. A relative, perhaps an in-law, knows someone who can help you get ahead. If you have something to sell, a neighbor or local shopkeeper might buy it. Money will find its way to you, just when you need it.

Saturday the 22nd. Both kindness and criticism are in the air today. You could be floating above it all, high on love and hope. This day is built for glitter, tinsel, and fantasy. Creative decorating for the holiday should be inspired. Your wardrobe choices will be artistic and imaginative. A stressful streak is present, too, possibly the cause of a cranky spat and brief separation.

Sunday the 23rd. Spiritual beliefs and practice may seem more meaningful now. A profound conversation or thought-provoking literature could result in an epiphany. Attending a holy place of any variety will likely appeal to the devout Scorpio. An incredible Full Moon graces the night with high emotional energy. Bold Scorpions are sure to rev up the partying.

Weekly Summary

The saying that life is a box of chocolates might be appropriate now. Cosmic diversity augurs many differing and notable occasions. People networks, both personal and professional, may ramp up. Communications increase, with lots of mail, invites, calls, and encounters. Conversations may go on and on, but your mind can stay as sharp as a tack amid the rising tempo. Knowing when to stop is key.

You may adopt a too serious perspective. When the people around you express dour thoughts, it's vital to listen with a third ear and read between the lines. Otherwise, you might jump to erroneous conclusions. Many Scorpios could discover just how effective your famous powers of persuasion really are.

The weekend brings the solstice, the last seasonal turn of the year, with the Sun entering Capricorn on Saturday. Sunday night's beautiful Full Moon in Cancer is friendly to all water signs, especially yours. It's time for a well-earned break.

52nd Week/December 24–31

Monday the 24th. Relax and enjoy if everything is in order. If you left arrangements until the last minute, you will have your work cut out. But some superhuman level of running around can still get things done. Local and international transit might suffer frustrating breakdowns and organizational dilemmas. When it's all over, a better humor settles in to welcome Christmas Eve.

Tuesday the 25th. Merry Christmas! Past pressures should be nonexistent on this holiday. The heavens flow nicely for Scorpio. Those of you at the helm of any celebrations can have particularly delightful moments amid the busyness. Serious conversations are likely, especially with older folk or an overseas visitor. Pleasing and being pleased are the themes voiced in unison.

Wednesday the 26th. It is a high-power day, physically, emotionally, and intellectually. Scorpios off work may attend yet another boisterous party. Those of you back at work might be fielding arguments and confrontations. Errands, short trips, and calls will keep you busy. Longer journeys undertaken now will be successful.

Thursday the 27th. Scorpio travelers may return to familiar territory, perhaps connected to a prior achievement. A name on an honors list could hold much meaning and offer inspiration for later things. Consult another relative about a sibling's recent antics. Keep any intervention within the family unit for now. Kinship proves vital when a loved one loses the plot and strays from the path.

Friday the 28th. Scorpios back in the world of work, at home or at business, will return with a vengeance. If something has to get done thoroughly, you will do it. Extra gumption will lead to extra gain. A jovial friend is really quite realistic and an excellent coach. Take heed of commonsense advice. If you are on vacation, enjoyable trips and encounters lift your spirits.

Saturday the 29th. Friends, partners, and associates can contribute to social times. Quirky and unexpected occurrences can carry surprising good fortune. A youthful individual has information worth hearing. This could include words from the mouths of babes. Sulking in silence while a loved one dumps blame isn't smart or useful. Open up, heart to heart.

Sunday the 30th. Better separate the sheep from the goats in a group. Who is solid about a commitment versus who is not can be the catalyst to get people judging. Earnest friends will hold their ground stoically, sticking to the plan. A loved one may be leaving to go off somewhere, which warrants a last rendezvous. Bittersweet might become the tone of the hours.

Monday the 31st. Borrowing money to have a good time might be unavoidable. Of course, you will pay later. But the clever Scorpio can always find exactly what is needed. A conference with a neighbor is wise if you are planning a big home event. An exclusive, private environment will appeal if you prefer subtle and low-key. You may reflect deeply on the end of an affair.

Weekly Summary

Mars, your coruling planet, starts this period still retrograde in Cancer. Days can fill with much action and energy. One landmark event may mark the season, aside from or within the obvious celebrations. Knowing where you stand with someone is the week's big revelation.

Moving around, connecting with people, and traveling are indicated. If you can't get away, at least call and write friends and associates afar. Visits and stays are likely, especially with siblings, aunts, and uncles. Interaction with neighbors, local shopkeepers, and even tourists in your area might feature. Social diversity is highlighted.

On Sunday Venus leaves Scorpio and enters Sagittarius. On Monday retrograde Mercury slips back into Gemini. Lots of thinking is in the cards, quite possibly about unfinished business. Here is a second chance to act upon certain information, to seal loose ends. When old doors are really closed, then the wonderful potential of 2008 will show itself. An adventure awaits. Happy New Year!

DAILY FORECASTS:
JULY–DECEMBER 2006

Saturday July 1st. Eagerly anticipated plans for a weekend away with friends may be derailed. Quick thinking can save the day, possibly providing interesting detours and new acquaintances. A spontaneous get-together can lead to career offers or other opportunities.

Sunday the 2nd. A devotional service or a community gathering will bring together a diverse group sharing common beliefs. A sense of wanting to belong will gradually subside into a need for private time. Someone from your past comes back to haunt you.

Monday the 3rd. Staying at home in cozy circumstances, preferably with a desirable companion, is today's optimal choice. However, you may need to make a command appearance whatever mood you're in. Polite dignity can calm and soothe the crankiest characters.

Tuesday the 4th. A combination strategy of gallant forthrightness and financial generosity can win hearts if not minds. Do not expect total honesty and forthrightness from some you're dealing with. Peel away the veneer of their charm to see the real deal.

Wednesday the 5th. Don't expect flexibility or compassion from anyone in authority, no matter the cause or circumstances. Exuberant personal aspirations can clash with career and family commitments. Choosing to please yourself over others may seem selfish.

Thursday the 6th. What starts out harmlessly can lead to tricky challenges. You may need the help of those in high places if your reckless behavior has led to hard consequences. Foolish vulnerability can lead to disappointment or a betrayal of trust.

Friday the 7th. Following your good Scorpio intuition can pay off on the job or in the field. Salespeople will attract serious business. Personal promotion should enhance your reputation and standing. Keep in mind that it takes money to make money.

Saturday the 8th. When it comes to attaining your heart's desires, rushing in where fools fear to tread will have unexpected consequences. On the other hand, in matters of love and money there might only be time for a quick decision. Just proceed with cautious haste.

Sunday the 9th. Loaded issues can be addressed in the most positive ways. Kids will benefit from a reality check on the cost of living and the real value of toys and games. Gambler's debts must be honored. Obsessing over a forbidden relationship can be expensive and risky.

Monday the 10th. Formal correspondence and reports are front and center today. Whether the audience is simply the boss, peers, students, or remote officials, deliver any communication with dignity. Being responsive and spontaneous is vital.

Tuesday the 11th. Being taken the wrong way, or inflicting that on other people, is easy in the wake of the overnight Full Moon. Check details, read critically, and review understandings before making any irrevocable decision. Remain open to new input.

Wednesday the 12th. Where you live, who you live with, and how you go about living there are of supreme significance to both your job performance and your personal well-being. Make things right at home and everything else will proceed and progress.

Thursday the 13th. Your dedication and effort are paying off, possibly with larger earnings than expected. You may be in a position to invest in property. Serious dreaming and consideration could be directed at starting or providing for a family.

Friday the 14th. This freewheeling, fun-loving day comes as a refreshing change after the rigors of sterner circumstances. Financial risks, taken with jaunty confidence, may prove highly valuable. Spending on treats for a loved one or child is a natural loving gesture. Be as generous as current circumstances allow.

Saturday the 15th. Persuading a group to go along with your view in an important matter involves politics and psychology. If there's a choice, go with the crowd. At close quarters mutual energy may be extreme, as a relationship becomes a life-or-death scenario whatever the actual circumstances.

Sunday the 16th. Physically demanding household chores should top your to-do list. Routine exercise with aerobic exertion and gravity-defying antics will be healthful. Burn off calories in useful activities. A weekend job search should pay off.

Monday the 17th. Transportation and delivery delays could hold up an institutional project or corporate endeavor, creating circumstances that lead to a legal dispute. A key associate or employee might be traveling and unavailable, or be out of sync with the plan.

Tuesday the 18th. A passionate period in a relationship has reached a point of preparing for broader horizons and more expansive experiences. Second thoughts about joint plans might be triggered by the need to juggle individual needs against mutual expectations. This conflict is likely to lead to either all in or all out. Let any first move come from the other person.

Wednesday the 19th. Slipping out of work commitments or taking advantage of lax supervision might be a temptation for the lazy and unscrupulous. Far horizons appeal. Whatever guilt or regret you know might follow, it could seem worth it to spend the day in relaxed conversation; have an excuse or alibi prepared in advance.

Thursday the 20th. Family ties can be renewed when a relative arrives from overseas. A phone call could fill important blanks concerning the health and fortunes of immediate family members and dear friends. Experts you consult will be knowledgeable and reassuring.

Friday the 21st. Long-distance love might be all that's available to you right now. If your partner is away, a phone call will be welcome comfort. Scorpio singles could find it easy enough to hook up while cruising alone. A romantic date needs the right setting to be truly impressive and memorable.

Saturday the 22nd. A grouchy start to the day, or any early unpleasantness, shouldn't deter later plans for an outing or party. Get all the shopping out of the way first thing. Parents and children may clash due to differing agendas and perspectives, but all's well that ends well. Caring affection and goodwill lead to happy outcomes.

Sunday the 23rd. Despite a natural inclination to focus on your private life and personal growth, this is a time to get involved with the world and everyone in it. Challenges like water-skiing, surfing, or sailing would be exciting for the uninitiated and skilled alike.

Monday the 24th. Important, pivotal communications could be on the desk or in the mailbox. Events are moving to a decision point throughout this week. To get ready, make all necessary preparations without jumping the gun. Listen carefully and think things through. Some matters still need negotiation and final clarification before you initiate slow but steady progress.

Tuesday the 25th. Your public standing, reputation, and career advancement are all in the spotlight. A Leo New Moon may be too dry and too exposed for you to feel comfortable. Such discomfort can be harnessed as a reminder to aim for personal bests in career endeavors, and perhaps more broadly in life itself. Set goals.

Wednesday the 26th. Getting into gear may be a little slow, as if you're resisting the flow of life's necessities. Feel the sun on your head and the wind in your hair while effortless progress is made, at least with earning a living. Realists need a dose of shining inspiration.

Thursday the 27th. Actions need to speak louder than words, whether they're yours or those of other people. Gear up in anticipation of a flurry of energetic effort. Ignore the doubts or opinions of pessimists and cynics. Team tasks and group projects are now moving front and center, ready for permission and then ignition.

Friday the 28th. Whether to go it alone or be part of the crew might be a tough choice. Unless total freedom is essential, cooperative participation is the preferable path. The synergy that builds from collective knowledge and experience can be remarkable. Breakthroughs are heralded as novel approaches lead to solutions.

Saturday the 29th. Telling a truly annoying character how you really feel may have been a long time coming but is best expressed now. Finally you can get it off your chest. If the person is someone from the past who's been haunting you, stalking you, or just hanging around, make the cut permanent.

Sunday the 30th. Relax, taking pleasure and satisfaction in a job well done. Entertainment provided by an athletic contest or cultural display is sure to be enjoyable. Maintaining inner calm and poise is essential as you prepare for upcoming trials. Do not even think about taking the easy way out during the week ahead.

Monday the 31st. Getting involved where you aren't needed, wanted, or appreciated could have unpleasant consequences. Scorpio do-gooders be warned. Meaningful personal intimacies and close family ties take precedence over worldly affairs. You may develop a fascination for someone who doesn't know you exist.

Tuesday August 1st. The Moon enters Scorpio, auguring sufficient personal motivation when it comes to pursuing your aims. Friends and allies are important as you band together to achieve desired results. Much progress is possible if you exert the effort.

Wednesday the 2nd. Mixed blessings mark this day, potentially making for a bumpy ride at various points. Some kind of authority, either an individual or an organization, could get heavy-handed. What appears to be a setback could eventually turn out to be a boon for you.

Thursday the 3rd. Thought and talk of long-distance travel can dominate over actual action. However, if a trip relates to a child or to a lover, your reaction may be quite different. A valuable educational course may catch your attention. Do not hesitate to sign up.

Friday the 4th. An ambitious goal will be aided by a generous amount of grit and determination. Someone in a high place may be helpful, provided you offer the right respect. Scorpios who play the game well with bureaucracy may soon be movers and shakers.

Saturday the 5th. A hefty expense may emerge just when you don't have the money on hand. This can relate to a large investment such as a house or car. If symptoms of a cash crunch start to develop, do something about it soon. Look for little ways to economize.

Sunday the 6th. A public event taking place locally promises an amusing and interesting time. Scorpios who dare to be spontaneous and just go for it will be rewarded. Lucky surprises and surprising encounters are foreseen. Let loose with someone you love.

Monday the 7th. What you think will be a minimum of running around may take over the entire day. Pedestrian or vehicular traffic is apt to be busy. Any shortcuts are likely to turn into the long way around. For students, a study buddy may be an attractive idea.

Tuesday the 8th. Physical energy and personal confidence combine well to contribute to a meaningful group enterprise. Very boisterous actions may go over the top, as too much force is sure to produce damage. Home is the most likely venue for blunders.

Wednesday the 9th. Something sneaky may come your way, possibly connected to a housemate or relative. A person who is close to you may be annoyingly evasive or may act suspiciously, arousing questions. However, the Full Moon poses exposure of whatever is hidden, especially if it is deceitful. The law rules now.

Thursday the 10th. Romance, or infatuation, with an individual of some status is in the air. A new superior might arrive on the scene, provoking your imaginative dreams. A notable overseas theme colors the day, possibly the return of a loved one from far away. International lovers may appear intent on connecting.

Friday the 11th. For Scorpios whose love life recently experienced disruption or even a radical change, an ending appears to be part of the picture. This may mean it's all finished and fragmented. Or it may simply be that an aspect of the affair has ended, a natural part of a relationship's growth cycle.

Saturday the 12th. You may be entrusted by a friend or relative to transport a valued item somewhere important. A journey should flow well, particularly when a companion is by your side. Beauty and glamour, likely a public figure, has the potential to create certain wishes and galvanize you into action.

Sunday the 13th. Even everyday tasks and routines can be tackled with a more positive attitude. Leaving a personal stamp on even the smallest of tasks can lead to you being recognized and rewarded. A stirring encounter with someone who gives as good as they get can be the start of romantic attraction.

Monday the 14th. Competition and opposition lend a tense edge to the atmosphere. You may be directly involved, or just the innocent bystander as other people go at it. The workplace is the most likely battle arena, with words the weapons of choice. Be wary of spouting emotions that you never intended to reveal.

Tuesday the 15th. Social invitations and occasions could come your way. There might be a choice between a formal event and a more spontaneous casual affair. Pleasure and comfort are likely to rule over duty and tradition. Someone in charge could fall from grace, or at least their pedestal can start to wobble precariously.

Wednesday the 16th. As a Scorpio you are in line to gain added respect and standing as an individual in your own right. A substantial pay raise or some kind of kickback might be a reward for work well done. Selling art or other items from a legacy will be profitable. Scorpios in industries related to glamour and pleasure are in favor. You might get discovered or do some discovering.

Thursday the 17th. Kids are apt to manifest rebellion. Willful tantrums and unruly behavior might test the mettle of Scorpio parents or those working with youngsters. Your maturity should speak for itself in many circumstances. Recognize your limitations.

Friday the 18th. The dynamics of possession and doing the right thing may be entwined. Someone has to let go and cut the losses. Or it could be about mutual backing off. A legal battle related to closure can reach culmination or at least a major turning point. Any judgment is primed to be reasonably satisfying.

Saturday the 19th. Sharing good spirits with a loved one is likely to create more of the same. Enjoy today's exuberant mood. Adopt a don't-fence-me-in attitude. Unexpected good is apt to pop up out of the blue, offering enjoyable novelty. Don't be a couch potato.

Sunday the 20th. Serious pursuits and activities concerned with social responsibilities match this day. A political flavor might infiltrate events, especially public ones. Attending a long meeting or lecture may not appeal, but gems of gold lie among that leaden content.

Monday the 21st. This day is perfect for enjoying the theater of the otherworldly and imaginary, or at least a good movie. Your attention span is sure to waver when it comes to the real world, since yearning for something distracts. A loved one might receive a prize or valued recognition. Beauty and charm open a lot of doors, but not for free.

Tuesday the 22nd. Business expansion is sure to mean more running around and longer hours. Time for yourself or your family may have to be sacrificed due to work commitments. A social event with the boss or other higher-ups may require your attendance. A loved one could be miffed at not being invited.

Wednesday the 23rd. A swift commercial transaction may pay off, although probably on the small, even hidden, side. Notable new acquaintances can enter your life, bringing high hopes. A best friend may emerge as your relationship starts with a sense of familiarity.

Thursday the 24th. Little things definitely mean a lot, particularly in terms of measuring the worth and value of possessions, not to mention yourself. The eyes and judgment of experts are sure to be precise and incisive, pulling no punches. Apparently blunt critique will actually be well meaning and helpful.

Friday the 25th. A friend may be seeking backing for some kind of new investment. This person may become quite insistent and begin to press intolerant buttons. It's best to avoid being either a lender or a borrower at the moment. Will and power can clash big-time, either immediately or inevitably building over time.

Saturday the 26th. The challenge of presenting work loaded with private emotion to the public may confront Scorpio artists. Beauty is in the eye of any beholder, but the issue involves what is beautiful. If gearing up for any kind of talent contest, rehearse well. Just because your nearest and dearest say you're gifted doesn't mean everyone else is going to agree.

Sunday the 27th. Glamour and power are an ideal mix for Scorpios. Status is important today, and a rise in standing could await the deserving. Exclusive events may dot your social calendar. Mingling with the upper crust shows how the other half lives and plays.

Monday the 28th. A deal gone sour with an organization or institution could return to haunt and hassle you. Legal counsel could be needed, and will prove a good move if the dynamics of the situation intensify. Someone who speaks well may argue on your behalf, though you have a strong urge to fend for yourself.

Tuesday the 29th. Water signs, especially yours, are in line for lucky breaks and good clean fun. Risk takers and gamblers dance with Lady Fortune, and the chosen lucky ones are in for an auspicious tango. Knowing when to stop is the real trick to achieving your desires.

Wednesday the 30th. Tension underlying daily life may escalate to the bursting point. The more denial there has been, the more volcanic matters have become. Pressure needs to be released cautiously at a measured pace rather than in a flood of intensity.

Thursday the 31st. Negotiations and contracts regarding a purchase can be reviewed but not formalized right now. Money and talk are generally bad partners today. A friend might complain, thinking that you have somehow ripped them off. Do whatever is necessary to restore harmony. Someone else may sting you, even if it's with the most good-natured of intentions.

Friday September 1st. Upwardly mobile Scorpios could get an opportunity to climb a few rungs up the social ladder. Connecting with the right person is the key. Be quick to accept an exclusive invitation which offers some kind of prestige. An important introduction is possible. Money and power are speaking loud and clear.

Saturday the 2nd. Daring to be a little left of center might have tongues wagging and produce defensive reactions. Do all in your power to remain objective, refusing to buy into what's actually an issue for other people. The best coach today is yourself.

Sunday the 3rd. The focus is on your good friends and other acquaintances. Long-term familiarity can settle into agreeable exchanges among a diverse group of individuals. You may also opt to latch onto that one special sidekick and strike out in pursuit of a good time. The day is geared for play and satisfaction.

Monday the 4th. The desire of a loved one to be more independent and to do something different could lead to an urge for private space. Separation can be in the wings, possibly mutually. Apartness isn't just about some kind of aloof standoff. Individual needs must have room to emerge beyond intermingled feelings.

Tuesday the 5th. Some days are more stressful than usual, but they always pass. Today a variety of directions will pull at you. Sticking points relate to your home life, career, and personal liberty. Seeing only limitations and frustrations is easy. In the extreme, you could go overboard emotionally, requiring time out.

Wednesday the 6th. News concerning a special friend, perhaps an ex-partner, could stir up a lot of talk. This person might be returning to the vicinity and possibly reconnecting with a group of mutual friends. The choice is whether you should get involved all over again or keep your psychic and physical distance.

Thursday the 7th. The unexpected is somehow to be expected. Upbeat astrology graces a promising Full Moon. Fortune and even a small windfall might grace the chosen. Enjoy exclusive quality time with that special person in your life.

Friday the 8th. The true nature of a financial situation could have you feeling bleak. The fine print may be finally emerging, proving what is really going on. Damage control, if needed, should be engaged in right away. Keep close track of day-to-day expenses.

Saturday the 9th. What may initially seem daunting due to sheer necessity can turn out to be a blessing in disguise. Once you take a situation or problem by the horns and start to turn it around, validation will ensue. The universe supports your good decisions.

Sunday the 10th. Good services and products should be paid for in full, plus an occasional bonus given or received. Other people appear capable of offering excellent assistance and skills, as quality rules over quantity. A special item might have to be purchased, or at least put on layaway. A gathering with friends sees your companion truly charm everyone who is present.

Monday the 11th. Some Scorpios can't seem to turn off the magnetism even when other people come clamoring for attention. Differing people from various facets of life will all be packed into the day's experience. Boundaries and priorities are apt to be tested, since one person may have overstepped the mark. Not everyone can be kept happy all of the time, but you can try your best.

Tuesday the 12th. If you pick someone's brain today, an influx of information is apt to emerge. A colleague knows important details which will aid in settling an agreement with a third party. Specialized, rarified activities are favored. Behind-the-scenes accomplishments please those who count.

Wednesday the 13th. Greed has a way of fragmenting certain associations. Trying to reach an important agreement can be stymied by polarized opinions regarding profit and loss. A group may have one idea while an individual thinks something completely different. It could be you who wants to take the path less favored. A spiritual person may offer unconditional aid.

Thursday the 14th. A person of authority, or at least in a respected position, will be of immense help sorting out an issue concerning shared resources. The voice of reason will be well expressed when the right specialist is consulted. The stars support linking with professionals and being prepared to accept what they have to say.

Friday the 15th. There's a buzz in the air for those who choose to listen. Change is today's keyword. Obtuse facts may appear ever more interesting as the unusual grabs your attention. Scorpios who are into anything zany or lateral should be flying high.

Saturday the 16th. Scorpio students pursuing an ongoing path of higher learning are about to hit some type of benchmark achievement. Moving into a place of greater understanding will enhance your self-esteem on a very personal level. Knowledge, or just acting with wisdom and consideration, leads to success.

Sunday the 17th. This initially laid-back day could mutate into a big day out, even if you start a little late. The world is there for you to experience. Activity may continue well into the wee hours, especially if you are in a group attending a large public event.

Monday the 18th. Old associations with your past may be caused by an invitation to a school reunion. Heritage and history attract your interest, getting the detectives in the Scorpio pod off and running. You may be torn out of your preferred comfort zone due to extra responsibilities that cannot be put off any longer.

Tuesday the 19th. A pleasurable social time is possible, likely in refined surroundings. Understated detail is the key if you are embarking on a makeover or fresh image. Money can be well invested in self-indulgences which will add to your growing charisma.

Wednesday the 20th. Surprise, or even shock, signifies the turning point of an affair. Quick, sudden events might disrupt proceedings, creating unavoidable adjustments. Avoid getting all rigid and controlling. What doesn't bend will likely break. The backing of a group of people will give you the confidence to take a well-calculated risk. A potential lover is on the horizon.

Thursday the 21st. Someone may be feeling generous and offer to pay your expenses. If choosing to accept such an offer, be clear on whether it's a gift or a loan. On the other hand, a magnanimous mood can descend on you if you have some excess funds. Share what you know as well as what you have.

Friday the 22nd. Today's subdued tone reflects a gentle New Moon. It's best for rest and recuperation. You might resolve to spend more personal time out and about. A changing of the guard is about to happen, replacing someone in a high position. Consider taking charge or at least casting your vote.

Saturday the 23rd. Scorpio athletes should get up early and go straight into the chosen activity. For others, it's just a case of floating back into the snooze position. Easy-flowing energy has a way of soothing away any cares, especially suiting lovers and aesthetes.

Sunday the 24th. A person who will be very helpful in achieving your ambitions and goals could be met visiting a friend. Arrange to be with individuals who possess ample experience. People respected for what they've accomplished can be the best role models. A temporary job is likely to add substantially to earnings.

Monday the 25th. Lightweight and heavyweight planets partner up like pairs of mismatched dancers, including a Moon in Scorpio. Definitive changes in tone, mood, and focus may be registered. These range from deep concerns to playful freedom. Hang on to your emotional hat and enjoy the whirlwind of change.

Tuesday the 26th. A tendency to exaggerate and overreach can lead to slipups. You may get careless, especially around the house. You might choose to please yourself, doing what suits you best. The consequences can be faced later, and there will be some.

Wednesday the 27th. Someone in the family, or a roommate, may retreat to a place of healing for a while. This sanctuary will surely be beneficial. Today favors pursuing remedies to virtually anything, including a financial fever. A tip may be passed on to you, promising easy money. If it's too good to be true, it probably is.

Thursday the 28th. A disagreement related to a rare object can be resolved in your favor, possibly because hidden connections are paying off. Bargains are available at present, likely unearthed in interesting places. Scorpio antique lovers and collectors are in for a memorable time. A rehearsal should lead to productive results.

Friday the 29th. A major deal could be sealed. A great gain or a significant loss is possible. Clear information and putting all cards on the table will be crucial before anything is set in stone. Otherwise you may end up being locked into a long-term situation that can break the bank. Be sure to guard your reputation.

Saturday the 30th. Hasty action, even in fun, may lead to an injury inflicted on yourself or another person. Some little mishap, from a cut finger to tripping on the sidewalk, can get you riled up emotionally. Anger needs careful management. Kids are natural harbingers of a better outlook if you're prepared to listen to them.

Sunday October 1st. A bit of healthy selfishness can be valuable when you decide to do whatever pleases you most. There's happiness in autonomy, ideally supporting a personal generosity of spirit as well. In being good to yourself, other people reap benefits as well.

Monday the 2nd. The family, or a familiar crew, could secretly band together and plan some type of surprise. You may be in on the act, with a parent figure the intended recipient. The stars favor a clandestine tryst and romance. A conversation will uplift your spirits.

Tuesday the 3rd. Keep yourself well grounded. Mists and veils should tend to lift as the day unfolds. A higher-up professionally or socially may step in, possibly taking over control. Someone at home could be disgruntled about their own lack of power and influence.

Wednesday the 4th. The stuff of dreams is potentially successful if you follow through. A relative may offer thoughtful and compassionate guidance just when you need it most. New ground is broken through a heart-to-heart talk with a loved one.

Thursday the 5th. What begins as a fun encounter or event could mutate into serious business and deep concerns if issues of safety and security take the helm. A choice exists. Cultivating the right attitude is vital. A landmark occurrence related to a youngster is foreseen.

Friday the 6th. You must decide whether to stand up or back down. Someone of high rank could pull rank with inappropriate lordliness. Objectivity and diplomacy might be rare commodities although much needed. A cooling-off period would be your best bet.

Saturday the 7th. An otherwise very pleasant time could be marred by a grouchy attitude, so get with the program. A place promising collective fun offers heaps of satisfaction. Scorpio workers will benefit from solid returns if prepared to meet a challenge.

Sunday the 8th. This is an excellent day for connecting with that special someone and engaging hand in hand in a novel pursuit. A healthy sense of risk and exploration is in the air. Cyber fun beckons, especially if you are eager to establish new contacts. Strange facts will fascinate you and could open new vistas.

Monday the 9th. If you are attempting to keep involved simultaneously in many activities, you are likely to feel the stress. Key individuals from conflicting arenas of life may demand attention. Some judicious pruning to your schedule staves off irritation for one and all.

Tuesday the 10th. There's ideal astrological fodder for Scorpio artists, spiritualists, and all sensitives in general. Inspired creative ideas abound. Innovative approaches may lead to a whole new attitude and a more universal philosophical view. Entertaining and romancing your mate or a new love could prove very special.

Wednesday the 11th. Quietly chipping away at a task behind the scenes can produce outstanding results. Deserved recognition will boost both your personal status and your bank balance. The good graces of people within an institution or bureaucracy are important to cultivate. A family connection, possibly to an elected or appointed official, might offer opportunity.

Thursday the 12th. Do not hesitate to get involved with a unique or exclusive activity. Entrance into specialized realms can be pursued. Access could be granted to go backstage at a public event. Or you could actually be a participant in this kind of happening. Scorpios who are dealing in glamour and illusion are in for special recognition based on current accomplishments. Aim high.

Friday the 13th. As a water sign you will be generally blessed today, with fortune smiling on the chosen. Your personal magnetism, plus personal sensitivity, are the keys to getting what you want. Someone's wise words will finally crystallize into true comprehension.

Saturday the 14th. Keep your temper. Something is apt to make you cranky, so a cooling-off period would be wise. Conversely, if you seem to be wearing the kick-me sign, stand up for your rights. Throughout the day you will be hard-pressed to maintain a totally smooth and even keel, although life rocks less as the hours get later. Stay focused on long-term goals.

Sunday the 15th. Wily Scorpios need to sharpen wits and hone reflexes. Be on your toes as charlatans come to trap the unwary. You may become just as slippery as anyone else. When the subject is money, be on guard. You could be stung or caught in a sting.

Monday the 16th. Try to stabilize a relationship with the boss or with another individual in control. A balance of frankness and diplomacy will produce the best outcome. Keeping your enthusiasm in check and acting with dignity will be necessary as a way to impress conservatives. Remain faithful to a goal or responsibility.

Tuesday the 17th. Powerful work may be done on behalf of an institution or some type of charity. Scorpios who are working in, or dealing with, hospitals and healing services can expect a memorable moment or two. This evening, gremlins are capable of entering the picture in the guise of youngsters.

Wednesday the 18th. Any creative Scorpios, especially artists, designers, and musicians, may be bursting to express something beautiful. An increase in your personal worth means the prices for your creations will improve. Having to speak out could be unavoidable but very appreciated by those who need your support.

Thursday the 19th. Someone or something coming back from your past may haunt you. And old debt may be related to unfortunate circumstances. These fears prove unfounded when the nostalgic turns into an empowering event. Be ready to forgive and forget.

Friday the 20th. A timeless feeling encourages lost hours as you experience bouts of reverie. Going to bed early can lead to an influx of symbols in dreams. If your schedule is overly full today, cancel all but what's most important and intriguing.

Saturday the 21st. Moonlighting at a secondary job for a while will help you reap benefits. Or this activity could add an extra feather to your cap and put you in line for a future promotion. A sensual New Moon reflects evening activity geared for fun and romance.

Sunday the 22nd. It's feel-good time, promoting fun and pleasure. The shackles of duties, and hopefully any worries, can now be dismissed. Romance is in the air. Many Scorpios could experience a sense of getting into the magnetizing zone. A spontaneous affair may be triggered with just the right comment.

Monday the 23rd. Important cosmic gears shift. This happens all within the Scorpio sector of the heavens. Turn attention to yourself, whether through your own regard or that of others. Some type of coming out could be in order after a major revamp. Dress to impress. Consider a new hairstyle or color.

Tuesday the 24th. Yesterday's trends escalate as decorative Venus also slides into your zodiac sign. Personal image is ever more important. Self-indulgence can be hard to resist. The acquisition of anything that gratifies you and enhances your look may seem unavoidable. It could be that retail therapy has kicked in to soothe feelings hurt by a rejecting comment.

Wednesday the 25th. Planets of love and lust entwine in the heavens. The day is fantastic for lovers and for expressing passion. You will be electric with charisma but might not realize just how attractive other people think you are. Then again, too much vanity can take away your advantage.

Thursday the 26th. Your words could have a profoundly lasting effect on a family member, particularly a youngster or someone else you love. Strong truths have a way of being spoken unintentionally, possibly in jest. A big deal or a big bill is in the wings. Power and security take center stage. A notable event may take definite form.

Friday the 27th. Small pleasures and strokes of luck are foreseen. Feeling truly confident and comfortable in your own self attracts positive experiences and perhaps even romance. Affectionate words and charm can guide a relationship. Be alert for love. Acquiring material goods should take a backseat to socializing.

Saturday the 28th. If you're not being romanced or at least delightfully distracted, something has to change. Continue improving your exterior image. Feeling pleasure-challenged may not be realistic but nevertheless hard to overcome. Get out of a rut tonight.

Sunday the 29th. Being at odds with someone on the domestic front could be a growing concern. Differences of opinion as well as their irritating ways can get under your skin. You are apt to go on the defensive simply when pursuing the right thing but being confronted. Even the quietest Scorpio may tend to boil over, especially if a past issue arises yet again.

Monday the 30th. Domestic tension continues. One person can be acting helpless while another is taking too much control. But all want to change the situation. Breakthroughs are foreseen if you become proactive and refuse to take no for an answer.

Tuesday the 31st. Taking part in an enjoyable event or activity will lift your spirits markedly. Lovers and buddies can all contribute to the pleasure via a party for two or more. Energy can be happily burned, physically, mentally, and emotionally. Take pleasure in the soul of a magical Halloween.

Wednesday November 1st. An ongoing argument with bureaucracy can reach the ultimate point where enough is enough. Off-the-record negotiation involving you and a supervisor should result in a solution you can live with. You may charm someone silly, or be charmed in turn, through a most unusual chain of events. You'll encounter unexpected activity perhaps related to a child.

Thursday the 2nd. Any outstanding debt, bill, or loan may have to be repaid promptly now. Pay up whatever is overdue. Do all in your power to avoid hurting your credit record. Opportunities to socialize in your comfort zone are likely to be tempting.

Friday the 3rd. Innate, insightful feelings shouldn't be ignored when strongly exerted. This is particularly true if they pertain to home, family, and especially to youngsters. Intuitive capacities are latent in every water sign and may now become more effective. A mystical pursuit might catch your fancy and send you exploring.

Saturday the 4th. Ideally, you will transform and renew rather than create more madness. The heavens support those prepared to roll up their shirtsleeves and apply elbow grease. Hard work may flow with ease, especially if you're working with a friend.

Sunday the 5th. The urge to be like a hermit and hide out at home is strong, but at the sacrifice of fun. An individual with a strong bond to you can bring a sense of excitement and the unusual. Generally you have a way of getting spontaneous and excitable, especially if about a good time. Children should be full of energy.

Monday the 6th. You and a close associate may face a prior antagonist, whether it's a person or some type of organization. Determined Scorpios are likely to encounter equally determined opposition, leading to a standoff. Shared resources could be up for grabs, but don't give away what is rightfully yours.

Tuesday the 7th. Take a good hard look when a loved one or household member again pushes personal boundaries. This may involve the kind of company that's invited to your shared home. Someone might be adopting strays, which upsets your space and privacy. Do your best to find a compromise.

Wednesday the 8th. Getting to know a new friend will prove very interesting. Second looks and second thoughts are foreseen, plus you'll be scrutinized as well. Sexual magnetism and initial excitement can distract from the reality of a relationship. Money or an expensive gift may put you in an awkward position.

Thursday the 9th. Scorpio athletes and spectators of physical pastimes are highlighted. A breakthrough in scoring a personal best or learning a new skill can create pleasant surprises. Vitality should be high. Someone close appears not to comprehend the true nature of a request you make.

Friday the 10th. Luck, love, and bounty all connect today with lots of positive feeling. Optimism and self-esteem are on the increase as people pay close attention to you. A moment of great personal growth could be very pleasant. Enjoy a mutual admiration club with that special loved one. Indulge every whim.

Saturday the 11th. The consequences of previous actions and words may return to haunt you. Dwelling in nostalgia might lead to feeling sorry for yourself. Try to stay in the moment. Self-review could be enforced when a more authoritative type pulls rank and tells it like it is. Listen closely and you'll learn.

Sunday the 12th. A decision relating to changing your residence, possibly to follow a special aim, may make you feel stuck. Only you can resolve such a choice, although a loved one will offer good feedback. It's a day to appraise rather than be decisive.

Monday the 13th. The early part of the day might find you overloaded, with obligations that restrict personal freedom. Discipline is required. Plans for pleasure may have to be put on hold. Anticipation of more enjoyable pastimes can make completing tasks a challenge.

Tuesday the 14th. Mental and nervous energy can be heightened, with much rushing around and interacting. You can deal effectively with groups and organizations. Embracing enterprise will help move things along. A friend could ask for you to mediate a conflict.

Wednesday the 15th. For those born with the Sun in Scorpio, the charisma fairy is waving her wand. Excellent astro lineups augur generous spirits and social delights. Look forward to auspicious and beneficial events, or at least one major good time. If you've got it, flaunt it.

Thursday the 16th. Staying under the radar and keeping other people in the dark is a natural instinct for most Scorpios. This is a skill to draw upon at present due to your desire for privacy and time out. Or at least opt for a hassle-free day where everything is under apparent control. Staying at home, or retreating to some kind of serene removed environment, will prove most suitable.

Friday the 17th. A somber mood might throw a pall over the earlier hours of this day but is set to pass. Rumblings of a turning point in a drawn-out review might begin to be felt. Nonetheless, if you are on tenterhooks about receiving key information you still have to sit it out for a while. The patient and selfless are in line to be satisfactorily rewarded.

Saturday the 18th. You can now pursure solitude or a desire to take on any solo activity. There is a subdued edge to the start of the day. Operating in a private world is sure to appeal to Scorpios. Stoic as you may be, you still require regular times of withdrawal. Sometimes you have to pamper yourself.

Sunday the 19th. You may finally receive a delayed message or be able to send a document smoothly. Take advantage of the gifts of communication plus clever dexterity. Coordinated action will reap good results. A wish is apt to be granted out of the blue. Reliance on a family member might prove a mistake.

Monday the 20th. The New Moon occurs in Scorpio. This is one of those days where moods and situations which are negative in the morning turn positive by sunset. Utilize the impulse to reach out. An auspicious phase in personal voyaging has been seeded. An affair might be the source or cause of a journey.

Tuesday the 21st. Raising your self-esteem will result from a good review of what you really possess. Possessions aren't just material baubles. What you have includes individual talents and skills, possibly some yet to be developed. Get discovering, or prepare to be discovered.

Wednesday the 22nd. Your personal prestige is good enough for you to assert something when everyone else just is quiet and does nothing. If symptoms show something unhealthy growing along with your income, take action right away. A major problem may develop from what now seems to be a small issue.

Thursday the 23rd. The blues may see wind leaving your sails. This is just a sign of the times. Staying around the local area, close to your homestead, is preferred while getting on with what's necessary. Later, the phone or an e-mail can rev things up.

Friday the 24th. Interactions, exchanges, and an increase in activity should have the effect of making you engaged with the world and back in the loop. Neighborhood encounters are sure to be good-humored. There's a possibility of unexpected romance and delight right around the corner. Weird and wonderful skills can be displayed or learned. Enjoy the magic of the day.

Saturday the 25th. The camaraderie of a familiar clan proves its worth and weight in gold. Giving a special present may be part of the picture. Someone is likely to return the gesture in response to previous aid. An unconventional connection warrants an unusual date, but big expenses also seem in store.

Sunday the 26th. The magic of beauty and exotic design is likely to enchant your creative imagination. Scorpio craft workers, whether professional or hobbyist, can now produce work worthy of a hefty price tag. However, precious sentiment can weave into what you create now, making for attachments and no sale. Subtle silent messages appear more effective than any clever words.

Monday the 27th. A decision to pour resources and materials into a large construction of some kind may be erroneous. Exaggerated perspective is sure to lead to distorted perception. An objective and experienced individual is capable of sorting out confusion if you ask for advice. Redeeming past mistakes won't come easily or be cheap. Cut any losses.

Tuesday the 28th. Hitches and mistimings could wobble your applecart. It will pay you to pause for breath and take stock of weak links. Upsets and setbacks may mar smooth advancement. There's probably a good reason for any delay, although it's not initially clear.

Wednesday the 29th. Your endurance is enhanced by emotional motivation, a typical Scorpio talent. A tempting carrot dangled can be appealing enough to give you extra stamina and ambition to achieve. A bonus is available if you offer good, quick service.

Thursday the 30th. This is a great day for taking care of little tasks and chores. Even housework should be enjoyable. Encouraging developments concerning a coworker are likely. Giving positive reinforcement to valuable helpers will oil the wheels of progress.

Friday December 1st. The tough can get going, but the going doesn't have to be tough. Extra determination will support fantastic endurance. The Moon, Saturn, and Pluto strongly connect your sectors of money, work, and career. Devote most of this drive to getting ahead by moving mountains. Just check that you're not demanding too much of yourself or others.

Saturday the 2nd. Flippant comments and witty flirtation might spice up a normal event. With your gift of gab, you can impress a newcomer with unexpected attraction. Unusual methods and quirky approaches should be effective in opening many a heart. However, don't confuse genuine affection with a generous wallet.

Sunday the 3rd. An early morning argument may find you and your mate or another family member at odds. In any debate you and the other party are likely to stick to your own views. Agreeing to disagree, or to stay completely apart, may be the only way.

Monday the 4th. Expected growth in an investment may not have come about as expected, making you vulnerable for bills and debts. Evaluating your own current status against someone else's success will not put you in a good mood or fill the coffers. Guard against letting anyone diminish your self-confidence.

Tuesday the 5th. Dreams are rich with symbols of personal guidance if you can recall them. The emotional turmoil from recent opposition can lead to a deep tension. Your outward veneer can be maintained gracefully, however, as tact and peace prevail at any price. A mature person can help to stabilize your anxieties.

Wednesday the 6th. Respite is on its way. You should find the atmosphere becoming more receptive and less reactive, at least in terms of outright conflict. Excitement arrives, probably in the guise of someone or something unexpected. Open up to new amusements.

Thursday the 7th. Diplomacy and a smattering of allure can help seal a powerful deal. Beauty and brains may reap benefits, lending status in certain cases and bringing about change. Partnership manipulation and management can swing either to the positive or the negative. Talent spotters are out shopping today, and they're definitely after star quality.

Friday the 8th. Attention turns to what you possess or are likely to gain. This is a good day for sorting out finances and consulting a professional in the investment field. You can gain a lot of understanding about mechanics of the finances and the bigger picture.

Saturday the 9th. Your credit card could get maxed out before you know it. This is a better time to just window-shop. Seek inspiration for future purchases. With many sales being advertised and a range of prices for similar items, scouting around first will save money.

Sunday the 10th. People seen as holding the reins of power are likely to prove more understanding than they first appear. You will earn a lot of respect when greater wisdom leads to noble actions. A large donation may come to someone or some group in need, with you as the middleman. Holding strong beliefs and following through on your promises are the keys to success.

Monday the 11th. The previous day's exuberance carries into today. However, the ante may be up when the unexpected enters the mix. The spontaneous tone should increase, but a surprise could be seen as an interruption. Curb your excitement.

Tuesday the 12th. A friend having family trouble may seek your shoulder to cry on. You might even offer the couch for an overnight retreat. The situation will take on added tension when resources get low. Be prudent and balanced in setting boundaries. Honor what is dearest to your heart.

Wednesday the 13th. Certain resentment needs to be sorted out with a relative close to your age. Worth and value issues that have been ignored for a long time could be healed through a frank talk. Something positive is exchanged and validation is received. Small comments and gestures can mean a lot.

Thursday the 14th. Charity and compassion are highlighted at the moment, and these certainly begin at home. Altruistic Scorpio can go beyond the call of duty; opening the doors of your heart will be incredibly fulfilling on a spiritual level. Random acts of kindness have the potential to provide magic and love.

Friday the 15th. Being left on your own, with extra space and privacy, can lead to astonishing accomplishments. What seemed a daunting job could be relatively painless once tackled properly. Scorpios involved in construction and renovation are sure to be pleased with today's progress.

Saturday the 16th. Being free to move around on a whim is important in order to have a good day. This is likely, and in good company too. Shelve anxieties and shrug off obligations. The shadow of responsibility is around, but this isn't the day for being weighed down. Exploring a new direction is regenerating.

Sunday the 17th. Interrelating with a senior family member, especially a parent, could be a crucial aspect of this day. It's not a case of sacrificing what you want to do, but more a realization of the truly deep bond that exists between you. Reflect upon your personal heritage; memorabilia may stir deeper sentiments.

Monday the 18th. An important legacy item can come into your possession, but deciding what to do with it might not be simple. Athletic Scorpios could turn skills and talents into a healthy way of making a living. Explore your capabilities.

Tuesday the 19th. Loved ones may demand spontaneous action and offer bizarre ideas. The company of children should delight and surprise you. Scorpio singles might discover a love when a newcomer moves into the area, complete with the possibility of an unexpected meeting. Keep your hopes high.

Wednesday the 20th. A marked change in your income or some type of adjustment to your security could arise. The contributing circumstances are apt to be beyond anyone's total control. Greater powers may speak today, even the natural elements. Vulnerabilities in an investment should be addressed without delay.

Thursday the 21st. Great entertainment is foreseen in a totally uncontrived fashion. Something or someone alluring is in town, perhaps a former lover, maybe even a circus. Settling excitement down can be an impossible mission. You may attend a memorable event with a special person. It's not often that you have the chance to party like there's no tomorrow, so enjoy.

Friday the 22nd. With both the Sun and Moon in Capricorn, the day may be an oasis within a usually demanding time. But there could be no rest if you are still running around visiting or shopping. For Scorpios apparently in control, rest is best. Kick back at home.

Saturday the 23rd. You'll have energy to burn if you've paced yourself realistically during this past week. Or you may simply keep burning along, checking off your to-do list as you go and not worrying about what you're spending. Generous, high spirits see a party carry over to your place and be the start of something grand.

Sunday the 24th. You may be still at work. Hanging in there dutifully will earn you a little extra at least, but the rest of the world may disappear. Kind words are capable of being the most powerful and meaningful gifts. The art of listening is finely honed.

Monday the 25th. Merry Christmas! It's a time of presents and good cheer, but a truly extra-special item is certain to grace this day. It is likely related to deeply powerful sentiment in a thoughtful act or gesture of a close friend or a visiting family member.

Tuesday the 26th. A message or call from a relative highlights the day. A regular family tradition may be fulfilled or birthed today. This can involve a sibling. Neighborly attitudes and friendly, casual greetings may evolve to create a congenial gathering. Love abounds.

Wednesday the 27th. A serious oversight can see certain stuff lost, followed by a bout of tricky buck passing. You could be forgiven for thinking if something needs to be done right, you should do it. However, efficient aid will fix it all up, and no one will know.

Thursday the 28th. After a bit of a break, a lot of focus goes into everyday chores. Extra work might be taken on by Scorpios who are involved in service industries. Improvement and renovation are favored, making this day ideal for any kind of big cleanout.

Friday the 29th. A quick pleasure trip with your mate or partner is a possibility. A small journey offers the potential of inspiring a bigger adventure together at another time. Social networking and trading ideas should be fun as well as useful. Contacts pay off right now.

Saturday the 30th. Fixating on lack of achievement, or lack of anything, is the way to go nowhere. However, reflection may be a boon rather than a burden; self-pity can be dropped, leading to mobilization. Someone is hoping to get through to you.

Sunday the 31st. The outset of this day may be quite laid back, although a feeling of anticipation is present. The desire for romance and fantasy can grow, inspiring magical choices for tonight's celebration. Enjoy a good-bye to 2006 and a hearty welcome to the new year.

Star of Animal Planet's "Pet Psychic"

SONYA FITZPATRICK
THE PET PSYCHIC

She can talk to the animals.
Read their minds.
Diagnose their problems.
Heal their illnesses.
Find them when they're lost.
And offer comfort from
beyond the grave.
This is her story—and the remarkable
success stories of her "clients."

*Includes Sonya's 7 simple steps to
communicating with pets*
*Plus—practical information on care and feeding, emer-
gency preparedness, illness, moving, and introducing
new pets into the household.*

0-425-19414-0

Available wherever books are sold or at
www.penguin.com

WHAT DOES YOUR FUTURE HOLD?

DISCOVER IT IN *ASTROANALYSIS*—
**COMPLETELY REVISED THROUGH THE YEAR 2015,
THESE GUIDES INCLUDE COLOR-CODED CHARTS
FOR TOTAL ASTROLOGICAL EVALUATION,
PLANET TABLES AND CUSP CHARTS,
AND STREAMLINED INFORMATION.**

Cell Phone Psychics

Horoscopes to Your Cell Phone

Send a text message with your date of birth and get your personalized daily horoscope via text message to your cell phone every day for only $1.99 for a week!

Just Text TOTAL and your birthdate to 82020

If your birthdate is Feb. 15 1968 your message should look like this

TOTAL02.15.68 and be sent to **82020**

Text YOUR Message to a LIVE PSYCHIC

Send a Text message to one of our LIVE Psychics from your cell phone any time, anywhere Just text the word ISEE to 82020 and get the answer to that important question!

Dating - Just Text DATE to 82020

to find that "Special Someone" right on your cell phone!

Chat - Just Text CHAT to 82020

Make new friends, have fun stay connected!